SURRI
LORE AND LEGEND

Michael Lane

S.B. Publications

By the same author,
On the Trails of Sussex Writers
Songs of a Surrey Dog Walker

First published in 1999 by S.B. Publications
c/o 19 Grove Road, Seaford, East Sussex BN25 1TP

ISBN 1 85770 204 2

Typeset by **Pro Repro**, Bellwether Lane, Outwood, Surrey RH1 5QD

Printed by Adland Print Group, Unit 11, Bellingham Trading Estate,
Franthorne Way, London.

Front cover: *A Surrey cottage,*
by Helen Allingham (in the 1880's)
see page 88

Back cover: *Albury old parish church*

Title page: *Lingfield: the way to the church*

CONTENTS

ACKNOWLEDGEMENTS

The author wishes to thank the following who have permitted him to make reference to their published information and to use their illustrations: Outwood Local History Society, the Bourne Society, the Wealden Cave and Mine Society. He also wishes to thank Mrs Flint, widow of Peter Flint, for permission to use material from his book "RAF Kenley" (Terence Dalton, 1985)

INTRODUCTION

This is a personal miscellany, a collection of little pictures of Surrey people and places, some old, some not so old. Many other such books have appeared over the years; most are no longer obtainable, except for the occasional copy in a public library.

This is not a comprehensive history or guide-book. There are plenty of guide books in the shops that deal systematically with Surrey landscapes and antiquities, and my book is not intended to compete with them. This is a book to complement the conventional guide-book; it may be used to enliven books of walks, which are often devoid of commentary on the places they pass through. Or it may be simply an armchair book, to transport the reader to some of the many facets of Surrey's character and history.

The book is arranged, for simplicity, listing villages and towns that are the setting of my stories in alphabetical order. Admittedly, some accounts refuse to be pigeon-holed under one name alone and Pilgrims' Way just had to be given a heading to itself. I have tried to include as wide a range of places as possible, but angry readers in Carshalton, Cobham or Oxted may be disappointed because no entry appears under their local name. I am sure these places figure in many other books.

Few great houses or great churches are to be found in this modest landscape, although many middle-size country houses and old manors survive. But Surrey is more famous for the great buildings that have disappeared. There are ruins of once rich abbeys at Waverley, Newark, Chertsey, and - to backtrack to older boundaries - Merton and Bermondsey. Royal palaces at Cheam and at Richmond have been totally demolished. East Surrey has three demolished castles: at Starborough, Bletchingley and Reigate.

Surrey has obviously long been a place to have a country house within easy reach of London. There were Roman villas, no doubt well-connected by road to London. Much later, when roads were poor, notable country houses - but mostly modest - grew up. John Evelyn, whose relations had various properties in Surrey and who came finally to Wotton, seems to have travelled constantly in the late 17th century. But Surrey was still then largely a county of deep muddy lanes and small thatched cottages. With exceptions like Farnham (a bit of rare agricultural prosperity) and Epsom (the fashionable crowd from London) it was little touched by Georgian building development, and its little cottages were spared, to be immortalised by the painter Helen Allingham in the 1880s, before many were swept away or sanitised for our modern convenience.

Surrey's modesty extends to its industries - yes, industries! Glass, iron, cloth, gunpowder, mining of stone - they are all gone. Only the grotesquely ugly open-cast mining of sand, chalk (and fullers' earth - for cat-litter!) remains. Of the earlier activities there is little trace. Melodramatic history is also lacking - except for that memorable meeting at Runnymede in 1215. Revolution might just have started in Dorking in 1830, when much of Europe was ablaze - but it quickly died.

A brief word is needed to explain my choice of material. I have tried mostly to avoid retelling the too-familiar tales of history, and to use original material where I have it. There are stories of our own time or a generation before that should have their place. A bias may be detected towards the east of the county, which is where I live; but I have made many journeys to the west and to Guildford, so they should not be under-represented. I acknowledge my debt to the older writers like Aubrey and Evelyn, to some old local guide-books long out of print, and to local societies like the Bourne Society and my own Outwood History Society for pointing me towards some tales well worth telling or re-telling.

ABINGER

Bishop killed by rabbit

A stone cross stands in the Evershed Roughs - a patch of common ground near the village of Abinger Hammer to commemorate an event of July 1873. The land used to be part of the grounds of Abinger Hall, a Victorian mansion now demolished, but is now owned by the National Trust.

Abinger roughs
- memorial cross to Bishop Wilberforce

On that July day, Bishop Samuel Wilberforce was riding across country with Lord Granville (the Foreign Secretary). They were on their way from Burford Bridge (below Box Hill) to dine with Gladstone at the home of Mr Leveson-Gower at Holmbury. Bishop Wilberforce, you will recall, was the famous son of that famous father William Wilberforce, who campaigned for the abolition of slavery. Samuel, who was by all accounts a sensible and reforming bishop - first of Oxford, then of Winchester - has for us today a reputation for seeming ridiculous in his arguments against the truth of Darwin's ideas of evolution.

The bishop's horse caught its foot in a rabbit-hole. The rider was thrown. He was a heavy man, and fell on his head and was killed.

The stone cross carries the initials "S.W." and a bishop's crozier, and a commemorative plaque.

Abinger, Memorial plaque.

ALBURY

Myth maker

As you drive along the A25 between Shere and Newlands corner, you pass, at the foot of the downs, the Silent Pool. Alas, recent dry summers have rendered it a rather muddy, slightly dried-up pool. The name "Silent Pool" was given it by a writer of historical romances (and numerous other things), Martin Tupper (1810-1889), who created the legend of the pool.

His story - of a maiden pursued to her death in the pool by the wicked Prince (later King) John - has no historical basis. King John, however, was responsible for some murky deeds in Surrey, including the death in prison of Lady de Braose and her son, who lived near here.

Martin Tupper also lived close by at Albury. He was responsible for other Surrey legends that are simply ingredients of his historical romances. He wrote that before Magna Carta the scheming barons met in the caves

Albury old parish church

under Reigate Castle; that Archbishop Stephen Langton was born in Surrey, and had an affair with a local nun. But in his lifetime he was better known for another book, "Proverbial Philosophy", a book of couplets purporting to summarise wise advice for all occasions. The book was for a time immensely popular, but eventually fell from favour and even became an object of scorn.

But Tupper's Albury is well worth exploring. For a start, the village has moved. The mock-Tudor buildings with their tall chimneys that stand on the main village street are the 19th century creation of the owners of Albury. The original village with its ancient church, house and park stands away from modern roads, to the east. On the occasional days when the whole of the Park is open to the public, the area is a delight to explore.(The path to the old church in the Park is open at all times.)

The history is complicated. The splendid garden, with its long yew walk and its canal lying on the sunny south side of a little hill, was largely the design of John Evelyn, the diarist, tree-planter and land-owner in Surrey in the 1670s. It is sometimes open to the public at times in the spring when it is full of daffodils. This estate came into the ownership of Henry Drummond, wealthy banker, MP and man-about-town in 1819. The village was clustered round the old parish church and the manor house. But Drummond moved the village, closed the church and rebuilt the house. Not only did he build a new parish church where the new village grew up, but he built yet another church for his own sect, the Catholic Apostolic Church of which he was a leading member. It is this church you see as you approach Albury, turning off the A25 on the A287. This one is not open to the public, and the Catholic Apostolic Church is now just a historical curiosity.

These changes by Henry Drummond were stoutly opposed by Martin Tupper, who lived in Albury House. He claimed the right to be buried in the churchyard of the old parish church, but is in fact commemorated in both old and new churchyards. His grave is at the new one, but a family tomb outside the old one also carries his name. It is in this churchyard that Martin Tupper pictures the burial of the victim of the Silent Pool.

BLETCHINGLEY

Monumental pride

In the late seventeenth century Sir Robert Clayton was the dominant name in a large part of what is now Tandridge District in East Surrey, but little now survives except his tomb and monument. But what a monument! The late Jacobean and early 18th century funerary monument had a sudden and brilliant flowering, and Sir Robert's is one of the most extravagant. It fills the whole of the south transept of Bletchingley church, to the manifest displeasure of some of today's parishioners.

Inside a six-pillared Baroque archway that would not disgrace St Peter's in Rome, surrounded by cherubs, is placed a gigantic scroll recording the virtuous life of Sir Robert, and beneath it a more modest inscription to his wife. Life-size statues of husband and wife stand beside, one either side.

Bletchingley parish church - the magificent monument to Sir Robert Clayton

The monument was originally to his wife, who died in 1705, but he added himself to the monument, and it is his story that dominates.

The inscription is so splendid that it must be given in full:

"Here rests what was mortal of Sir Robert Clayton KT in the year MDCLXXX Lord Mayor Alderman and Father of the City of London and at his death near XXX years one of its representatives in Parliament.

"By the justest methods and skill in Business he acquired an ample fortune which he applied to the noblest purposes and more than once ventured it all for his country. He fixed the seat of his family at Marden where he left a remarkable instance of the Politeness of his Genius and how far nature may be inspired by Art.

"His relations, his friends, the hospital of St Thomas at Southwark (of which he was President), Christ Church Hospital and the Workhouse of London were large sharers of his Bounty.

"He lived in communion with the Church of England in perfect charity with all good men, however divided among themselves in opinion. The welfare of his country was the only aim of his Publick actions and in all the various Efforts that were made in his time for preserving the Constitution, he bore a great share, and acted therein with a constancy of mind that no prospect of danger could ever shake.

"It's but just the memory of so good a man should be transmitted to after age since in all the private and public transactions of his life he had left so Bright a pattern of imitation but hardly to be outdone."

Sir Robert did indeed acquire an ample fortune - he was the forerunner of the modern financial whizz-kid - banker, dealer in property, stockbroker, money-lender - and with his fortune came power in the City. The Dictionary of National Biography says of him starkly "bought Bletchingley, Surrey, 1677" - which means the whole manor, houses, farms and everything. Along with this he was MP for Bletchingley when he wasn't being MP for the City of London. As well as his magnificent house in London, he needed a house in Surrey, and so bought Marden Park, Woldingham from his friends the Evelyns, who owned large acres there and in Godstone.

The diarist Sir John Evelyn, also a Surrey man, related to the Evelyn who sold Clayton the Marden Park estate, describes in his diary a visit to the new mansion and park in Woldingham:

"From a despicable farme house Sir Robert had created a Seate of extraordinary expense. Tis seated in such a solitude among hills, as not being above 16 miles from London, seemes almost incredible, the ways also to it are winding and intricate.

"The Gardens are so large, and walled so nobly and the husbandry part made so convenient, and perfectly understood, as the like I had not seene... Innumerable are his plantations of Trees, especially Wallnuts, the Orangeries and Gardens very curious; large and noble rooms in the house...

"This place is exceedingly sharp in Winter, by reason of the serpenting of the hills, and wants running water, but the solitude exceedingly pleased me"

Alas, the house, with its noble rooms, was gutted by fire two centuries later in 1879, the lack of water no doubt contributing to its destruction. Only the stables survive, and the Victorian house that was built after the fire is now a convent school.

Sir Robert's monumental inscription, though florid, is carefully understated in one respect. Sir Robert's time was one of the most turbulent in our history; no sooner had the Civil War ended and the monarchy been restored than intense plotting and counter-plotting, religious strife, bloody execution, plague and fire devastated England. Treading a careful and principled path through the reigns of Charles II and James II was not an easy matter, and the inscription picks its way with care, with its references to defending the Constitution (i.e. keeping down the Catholics) and being in charity with all good men "however divided among themselves in opinion". Sir John Evelyn's diaries give a graphic record of how perilous the times were.

Perhaps surprisingly, a part from the tomb and monument, nothing remains of the Clayton name in Surrey - although back at the turn of the century, the "White Hart" in Godstone was called the "Clayton Arms".

Bletchingley parich church - a
medieval brass of the Trinity

What God looks like

A mediaeval brass in Bletchingley parish church contrasts, in its primitive lines, with the over-the-top Clayton memorial. It shows what God looks like - Father, Son and Holy Ghost (the latter as a dove) all comfortably ensconced in a great big throne.

BOX HILL

Invasion defences

It is difficult in our time to imagine the worries that our Victorian ances-
tors had that England was about to be invaded - by either the French or the

Box Hill - entrance to the fort.

Germans. Despite their confidence that the British Navy would defend the shores, there were periodic anxi-eties that London needed defences, and that the Surrey downs were the place for them.

There were such outbreaks of fear in the 1840s, and again in 1860 when a new French Napoleon declared himself Emperor. Then after Prussia had vanquished France in 1870 and appeared a dominating power in Europe, the new Germany became the imagined invader. The gap in the North Downs between Leatherhead and Dorking featured as a fictional battleground with the invader in a novel of 1871 - "The Battle of Dorking".

But fantasy later became a kind of reality. During the 1880s, partly because of a campaign by a retired army general, the Government again became concerned that Britain's traditional reliance on her navy for protection against invasion might not be enough. Bands of volunteers were raised and fortified assembly points were built along the north downs from Guildford in the west to Knockholt (Kent) in the east. Between 1889 and 1896, Army estimates show sums for the purchase of these sites - including five acres at Box Hill. Here was built a fort, with an embrasure for guns - but no guns were installed.

These remains are what can be seen now by every visitor to Box Hill. What is now a shop was once a barrack-room. But policy changed; a more powerful navy was built up. The land and buildings at Box Hill reverted to their original owners.

A similar structure can be seen on Reigate Hill, and another was erected on the west of the Mole Gap near Ranmore.

At least for a time these forts were actively used as mobilisation points. During the nineteenth century the Government at various times raised local militias for short-term service to supplement regular forces; towards the end of the century it began to raise "territorial army" volunteer forces, which became a considerable movement in the years before 1914.

BURSTOW

How much for an elephant?

Until recently, at Burstow Lodge Farm, next to a moated mediaeval house, stood a very large and tall barn. About 1990 it was demolished, and with it went the last physical remains of a remarkable era. The barn was big - to hold elephants, for here were the winter quarters of Lord John Sanger's Circus, from 1900 to 1941.

The Sanger circus family had a romantic history. The young James Sanger (born in Bristol in 1785) was visiting London as a young man. It is said that he saw a commotion a little way ahead of him as he walked on London Bridge, and before he knew where he was, it had enveloped him - and he found himself seized by a press gang and forcibly enrolled in His Majesty's Navy. Within hours he was on board a man-of-war and off to fight France at the battle of Trafalgar. Wounded, he was pensioned off and returned to Bristol - but his travels had brought him in contact with the

Burstow - Lord John Sangers elephants (about 1900)

arts of the travelling showman, and he had learned juggling. Soon he was on the road with a show - and the show grew into a full-blooded Victorian circus, carried on by his sons George and John. (A later poster maintains that the circus was founded in 1830). In time there was a full menagerie - elephants, lions and tigers, horses - and a kangaroo that was taught to box.

In 1871 "Lord" George and "Lord" John parted amicably and took separate circuses on the road. Then - as later - it was a gruelling routine of travelling from town to town, erecting the big tent, marshalling the animals and the acts, putting on just a few performances before taking it all down and trekking to the next town. All spring and summer long the routine would continue, and only in winter would they return to the fairly chilly hospitality of the barns at Burstow. Here rehearsal would go on to prepare the turns for the next year. (Someone who remembers the elephant barn says that there was a trapeze hanging from the roof).

A record of "Lord" John Sanger's circus in 1921 shows an itinerary of shows in 174 towns in England and Scotland, and 2000 miles travelled. The circus would start off in March, and hold a show first in Redhill, then in Dorking, then head north... That period, before and after the first world war, must have been the circus's heyday. But the second world war was its undoing. There were no more shows, and feeding the animals must have been a difficult and expensive business. There came a time when the animals at Burstow had to be dispersed to whatever zoo premises were looking after animals during the war.

A sale was held at Burstow Lodge in September 1941, with a catalogue listing animals and equipment. Notes in the catalogue record that an elephant was sold for 50 guineas - and the boxing kangaroo for 30 guineas.

There is also a strong tradition that in those wartime days before the sale, exotic animals used to be seen drawing the plough in the stiff wealden clay of Burstow Lodge farm lands. According to source, it was either an elephant or a camel. Alas , no-one was in a position to photograph this splendid sight, and we have only the local anecdote.

CAMBERLEY

A Town Renamed

Camberley was founded as a military training centre and given the name Cambridge Town, in honour of the Duke of Cambridge. He was a cousin of Queen Victoria and Commander-in-Chief of the Army from 1856 to 1895. However, the Post Office complained of the confusion caused by having two English towns called Cambridge, and the synthetic name Camberley had to be used instead.

The Duke opposed many of the reforms of the Army shown to be necessary by the deficiencies of performance in the Crimean War. An early tussle with Gladstone's government, when the House of Lords, the Duke and Queen Victoria were all very unsympathetic to the idea that the purchase of commissions should be abolished, was neatly sidestepped by Gladstone. Instead of having to introduce contentious legislation he discovered that much older legislation allowed such purchase only by royal warrant. He had the power - ironically on behalf of the Queen - merely to cancel it.

Eventually - but not until 1895 - the Duke was persuaded to resign, not before legislation had had to be brought in to make the Commander-in-Chief subordinate to the Secretary of State for War.

An old guide book says "the whole district... on the borders of Hampshire and Berkshire, abounds in wild tracts of heather and pine-woods, but is much spoilt by the straightness and frequency of the military roads."

CHERTSEY

Curfew shall not toll tonight!

The historical accuracy of the tale is doubtful, but Chertsey people have preserved the legend of the curfew bell; a local author, Albert Smith (1816-1860) who wrote for Punch, wrote it up as "Blanche Herriot: a Legend of Chertsey Church".

Blanche's lover Neville, the nephew of the Earl of Warwick in the time of the Wars of the Roses in the fifteenth century, had been captured by the Yorkists and condemned to die on Chertsey Mead. But he could hope for a reprieve if he could send a message to the king, with his ring as token. If a reprieve was not received by curfew time, he would die.

The message was sent, but the reply was delayed. The messenger was being carried across the Thames at Laleham ferry, as curfew time approached. This would be signalled as usual by the church bell. But the curfew never struck, for Blanche Herriot climbed the church tower and hung on to the clapper of the bell. The messenger arrived and Neville was reprieved.

CHIDDINGFOLD

Glass

> As for glassmakers, they be scant in this land,
> Yet one there is as I doe understand:
> And in Sussex is now his habitacion,
> At Chiddingfold he works of his occupacion:
> To go to him it is necessary and meete,
> Or send a servant that is discrete:
> And desire him in most humble wise
> To blow thee a glass after thy devise:
> It were worth many an Arme or a Legg
> He could shape it like to an egge
> To open and to close as close as a haire,
> If thou has such a one thou needest not feare:
> Yet if thou hadst a number in to store
> It is the better for store is no sore.

from Charnock's Breviary 1557

(Chiddingfold is of course near the Sussex border, but Surrey none the less)

CHILWORTH

Gunpowder and banknotes

"This valley which seems to have been created by a bountiful providence, as one of the choicest retreats of man; which seems formed for a scene of innocence and happiness, has been, by ungrateful man, so perverted as to make it instrumental in effecting two of the most damnable inventions that ever sprang from the minds of man under the influence of the devil!

namely the making of *gunpowder* and of *banknotes!* Here in this tranquil spot, where the nightingales are to be heard earlier and later in the year than in any other part of England; where the first a bursting of the bud is seen in spring, where no rigour of seasons can ever be felt; where everything seems formed for precluding the a very thought of wickedness; here has the devil fixed on as one of the seats of his grand manufactory; and perverse and ungrateful man not only lends him aid, but lends it cheerfully!

As to the gunpowder, indeed, we might get over that. In some cases that may be innocently and, when it sends the lead at the hordes that support a tyrant, meritoriously employed. The alders and the willows, therefore, without much regret, turned into powder by the waters of this valley; but the Bank-notes! To think that the springs which God has commanded to flow from the sides of these happy hills for the comfort and delight of man; to think that these springs should be perverted into means of spreading misery over a whole nation and that, too, under the base and hypocritical pretence of promoting its credit and maintaining its honour and faith!"

What splendid rhetoric! This is William Cobbett, recording his trenchant thoughts as he rides through Surrey in the early years of the nineteenth century. On the whole, for him agriculture was always good, city ways (and their demands) usually bad. But Chilworth, sitting in the little valley of the River Tillngbourne, was a centre for the manufacture of explosives until after the first world war. Today, little disturbs the peace of the riverside, which can be reached by public footpath.

CHURT

The Devil's Jumps - or are they?

William Cobbett, riding through his home county in August 1823, for once comments on something other than the state of the crops and the price of wheat:

William Cobbett - his Rural Rides included Chilworth and Churt

"At Churt I had, upon my left, three hills out on the common called the Devil's Jumps. The Unitarians will not believe in the Trinity, because they cannot account for it. Will they come here to Churt, go look at these "Devil's Jumps", and account to me for the placing of those three hills, in the shape of three rather squat sugar-loaves, along in a line upon this heath, or the placing of a rock-stone upon the top of one of them as big as a Church tower?

"For my part I cannot account for the placing of these hills. That they should have been formed by mere chance is hardly to be believed. How could waters rolling about have formed such hills? How could such hills have bubbled up from beneath? But, in short, it is all wonderful alike: the stripes of loam running down through the chalk-hills; the circular parcels tof loam in the midst of the chalk-hills; the lines of flint running parallel with each other horizontally along the chalk-hills; the flints placed in circles as true as a hair in the chalk-hills; the layers of stone at the bottom of hills of loam; the chalk first soft, then some miles further on, becoming chalk-stone; then, after another distance, becoming burr-stone, as they call it; and at last, becoming hard white stone, fit for any buildings... The clouds, coming and settling upon the hills, sinking down and creeping along, at last coming out in springs, and those becoming rivers.

"Why, it is all equally wonderful, and as to not believing this or that, because the thing cannot be proved by logical deduction, why is any man to believe in the existence of a God, any more than he is to believe in the doctrine of the Trinity?

"I got to Thursley about sunset, and without experiencing any inconvenience from the wet."

CLANDON

The serpent of Clandon.

"A serpent once infested a back lane in the parish of West Clandon for a long time. The inhabitants were much disturbed and afraid to pass that way. A soldier who had been condemned for desertion - promised, if his life was spared, he would destroy this serpent. Accordingly he took his dog with him. A fierce battle ensued, the dog fastened him and the soldier killed it with his bayonet in a field belonging to the glebe called Deadacre."

(An item in the "Gentleman's Magazine" of 1796.)

CROWHURST

Immemorial Yew

The church of Saint George at Crowhurst is old enough - dedicated in 1191, when George had just become England's patron saint - and before the crusades made him an even more popular patron.

But older far is the ancient yew tree close to the east wall of the church. Its leaf is green again in spring, but its trunk is a ravaged and splintered mass, some 33 feet in girth, exhibiting the punishment of the centuries - especially the recent ones. In 1805 it was hollowed out to make a room - there are various speculations as to its purpose - with a circular table and circular bench "capable of seating a dozen persons". A door to this room was fixed in the trunk. At that time a cannon ball was discovered lodged in the tree, thought to be a relic of the Civil War, of which a skirmish was fought close by.

In latter years the tree has been treated with more respect, its branches propped, its fungal attacks repelled. Very properly, its girth is measured each St George's Day. This seems to be still increasing slightly, if one compares the present measurement with records of 100 years ago. It has survived, with some damage, the hurricane of 1987, which blew strong in these parts; it has evidently survived that of 1704, and who knows how many before.

For the amazing thing is the tree's great age. Old guide books talk of speculation that it might be 1500 years old, taking us back to Saxon beginnings; the old guide books call this claim "extravagant". But the

Crowhurst - the yew tree thought to be 4000 years old

certificate pinned up in the church porch proclaims the tree to be 4000 years old! If this is to be believed, then we go back a mind-boggling distance in time - to the bronze age, perhaps, and the implications are fascinating. Clearly this was a sacred tree for many centuries - one thinks of Druids, whoever they were. Presumably it sowed itself from other yews, and as it grew venerable became itself venerated. The site must have long been a pagan shrine, before Christianity came here a mere thousand years or so ago. Consciously the church authorities decided to build their church here - on a small ridge, still pleasantly rural, but then looking out from its clearing into the great forest to the south.

In the next parish, Tandridge, the same thing : a yew also very ancient, though in much better shape, with its roots entwined in the Saxon foundations of the church. Holy ground long before the coming of Augustine.

CROYDON

The Oak's Revenge

John Aubrey tells this story of early environmental protest:

"In this parish lies the great Wood call'd Norwood, belonging to the See of Canterbury wherein was an antient remarkable Tree call'd Vicar's Oak, where 4 parishes meet in a point. This Wood wholly consists of Oaks. There was one Oak that had Misselto. Some persons cut this Misselto, for some apothecaries in London, and sold them a Quantity for Ten Shillings each time, and left only one Branch remaining, for more to sprout out; One fell lame shortly after; Soon after, each of the others lost an Eye and he that felled the Tree, about 1678 (tho' warned of these misfortunes of the other Men) would, notwithstanding, adventure to do it, and shortly after broke his leg as if the Hamadryads had resolved to take an ample revenge of the injury done to that sacred and venerable Oak."

DORKING

Travelling preacher

John Wesley (1703-91), the founder of the Methodist Church, spent a large part of his life travelling (mostly on horseback) round the country, preaching in the open air. Later, as Methodist "societies" were set up, and chapels opened, he visited them constantly. From a base in London, he often came to Surrey, and there are several entries in his diaries for Dorking, Leatherhead and Reigate.

He records visits to Dorking in 1764, 1770, 1772 and at the very end of his life, in 1790. At the beginning, finding that "the gentleman to whose house I was invited seemed to have no desire I should preach", he takes himself into the street:

"Friday, 13th January 1764. I went at noon into the street, and in a broad place not far from the Market-place, proclaimed the grace of our Lord Jesus Christ. At first two or three little children were the whole of my congregation, but it quickly increased, though the air was sharp, and the ground exceeding wet.. And all behaved well, but three or four grumbling men, who stood so far off that they disturbed none but themselves."

In 1770, he contrasts the people at Dorking with those at Reigate. At Dorking "the hearers were many, and seemed all attention. About a hundred attended at Reigate in the evening. and between twenty and thirty in the morning, dull indeed as stones." On another visit to Reigate, he has time to notice the Priory, and he describes in his diary the brief history. "The gentleman who possesses it now, has entirely changed the form of it; pulling down whole piles of ancient buildings and greatly altering what remains...The chimney-piece in the hall is probably one of the most curious pieces of wood-work now in the kingdom." The gentleman in question was the wealthy Richard Ireland, and it is at this time that Reigate Priory assumes the external appearance we now see facing the park. The chimney-piece in question is the building's richest jewel, said to have been brought from Bletchingley Place (another ruined palace) by an earlier owner.

But back to the more attentive Methodists of Dorking. Wesley opened their new preaching-house (he wouldn't have called it a church) on the 23rd of November 1772. Over the subsequent years he visits and preaches at both places:

"Wednesday 15th November 1775. I preached at Dorking; the next evening at Ryegate-Place, I think to the largest congregation that I have seen there; but still I think we are ploughing upon the sand: we see no fruit of our labours."

Years later we have these touching entries:

"Friday, January 1st 1790. I am now an old man, decayed from head to foot. My eyes are dim; my right hand shakes much; my mouth is hot and dry every morning. I have a lingering fever almost every day. My motion is weak and slow. However, blessed be God, I do not slack my labour. I can preach and write still."

"Monday, 25th January 1790. I went to Dorking, and laboured to awaken a harmless, honest drowsy people, who for many years have seemed to stand stock still, neither increasing nor decreasing."

(by the editor of his journals, filling in the last days):

"On Tuesday, (22nd February 1791) he went on with his usual work, preached in the evening at the chapel in the City Road [London] and seemed much better than he had been for some days. On Wednesday, he went to Leatherhead, and preached to a small company on 'Seek ye the Lord while he may be found; call ye upon him while he is near.' This proved to be his last Sermon: here ended the public labours of this great Minister of Jesus Christ." A week later he was dead, in his eighty-eighth year.

Revolution at Dorking

The summer of 1830 had been wet, and there was a poor harvest. The country was in depression, and elsewhere in Europe, revolution was

28

abroad. The wages of agricultural labourers had been forced down from five shillings [25P] a week to four and sixpence, or even, some said, to three shillings. This had to be supplemented by the dreaded "outdoor relief" - in which labourers were employed on public works schemes, like road mending, for an extra pittance.

A new threat to jobs emerged - the threshing machine, which would put out of work the hand-threshers with their flails. The countryside grew restive. Threatening letters were received by farmers and land-owners, often signed "Swing" or "Captain Swing". Ricks were set on fire, farmbuildings burned down, new machines smashed. By November, the south-eastern counties "had the look of revolution".

Among the farmers and gentry, stories began to circulate of well-dressed strangers being seen traversing the countryside, scattering mysterious warnings - these warnings being followed by "outrages".

On November 13, corn stacks were burned near Guildford; on the 14th Trouts Farm, Capel was attacked. And in the small hours on the 14th a miller at Albury was roused by furious banging at his door. He was also an overseer of the poor, and no doubt had some idea what was going on. As he cautiously opened his door, a gun fired at the downstairs room that he had just quitted, and in minutes his out-buildings were on fire, and his stores of corn and flour. When he appealed to the crowd to help extinguish the flames they are said to have replied : "Why should we? We can't be worse off than we are."

As the menace increased, the local magistrates assembled at Dorking on the 22nd to swear in special constables to maintain law and order. As they proceeded with this, gathered at the Red Lion, a crowd grew menacingly in the street outside. The High Street was full of labourers with bludgeons. They attacked the inn; threw a stone which knocked a magistrate senseless. But the Yeomanry arrived in the nick of time and beat back the crowd. The Riot Act was read, eleven rioters seized and taken to the Horsemonger gaol.

On the 25th a crowd at Woking determined to free the prisoners, and began to march on Dorking...but the revolution in Surrey got no further.

The marchers never arrived, but "slunk away, half-starved and miserable". Anyway, by a proclamation the army had been brought in. Significantly, the gunpowder works at Chilworth were well guarded. The turbulent year of 1830 subsided. Surrey has been pretty quiet since then.

EPSOM

Purgative Waters

Epsom must be one of the few towns in the world to give its name to a laxative - Epsom Salts. Epsom's place in history derives from a local discovery, said to be in the first Elizabeth's reign, that local people were deriving benefit from drinking the water in one of the small ponds on the

The source of Epsom Salts - the old well at Epsom, as seen early this century

common. "During the reign of James I, some physicians" (says the old County History) "visited the place, inquired into the facts and analysed the water, which they found to consist of a soluble bitter purging salt... the first to be discovered in England."

The active ingredient was magnesium sulphate; recourse to a medical formulary of our own day shows magntesium sulphate still listed as useful for the rapid evacuation of the bowel. However, the dilution to be found in the well on Epsom Common

30

(soon enclosed, and made a commercial proposition) made the water, according to Samuel Pepys, one of the gentlest and sweetest of the spa waters on offer in his time. He did note, of course, in his graphic way, that the ladies and gentlemen who partook of it disappeared soon after into the bushes...

But civilisation added to the drinking of the waters the provision of assemblies and entertainments. As early as 1640, there were visitors from overseas, and by the end of the 17th century Epsom was in its hey-day. Celia Fiennes, who published an account of her travels in England about that time, writes that:

"the Well is large without bason or pavement on the bottom; it [is] covered over with timber and is so darke you can scarce look down into it; its not a quick spring and very often is drank drye, and to make up the deficiency the people do often carry water from common wells to fill this in a morning (this they have been found out in) which makes the water weak and of little opperation unless you have it first from the well before they can have put in any other;... there is a walk of trees by it but not very pleasant, there is a house built, in which the well is... but it looked so dark and unpleasant, more like a dungeon, that I would not chuse to drink it there, and most people drink it at home; there are several good buildings in Epsome for lodgings and good gardens behind them for walking."

Even from Pepys' time, men used to lodge their families here and themselves travel up daily to the City; Epsom's history as a dormitory town had begun. As a spa it declined, but had the reputation as a place of fresh air away from polluted London. By the time Defoe wrote up his travels in 1724 or 1726 he emphasised the dormitory status:

"The greatest part of the men, I mean of the grave sort, may be supposed to be men of business, who are at London upon business all the day, and thronging to their lodgings at night, make the families rather provide suppers than dinners; for 'tis very frequent for the trading part of the company to place their families here, and take their horses every morning to London, to the Exchange, to the Alley, or to the warehouse, and to be at Epsom again at night; and I know one citizen that practised it for several years and scarce ever lay one night in London during the whole season."

Epsom's other claim to fame - the horse race - had to wait until 1790.

Farnham - the opulent palace of the Bishops of Winchester

FARNHAM

Princely Bishops

The wide main street rises nobly towards the castle, which looks out from its commanding hill to dominate the town and its river...

You could almost be in Salzburg, but the houses are solidly Georgian and English. But as so often across the patchwork of continental cities and provinces, this town was ruled by a bishop.

The bishop has been - until this century - the Bishop of Winchester, and a power in the kingdom. Farnham was usually his main residence. Winchester itself had a bishop in Saxon times, but became strategic for Norman and Angevin kings, since it lay close to the sea-route connecting their French dominions with England. And Farnham lay conveniently on the route from Winchester to London. From here the bishop, on behalf of the king, administered a territory from Taunton to Southwark, and south to the Isle of Wight.

In the troubled twelfth century, Henry of Blois was bishop when his brother Stephen landed to claim the throne in opposition to Matilda, Henry 1's only legitimate child. For Stephen, his brother's support was vital. When in 1138 Stephen offended his brother by not giving him the last step up the ladder to be Archbishop of Canterbury, Henry of Blois changed sides. He almost brought about a peace deal between Stephen and Matilda in 1141, but when it failed the civil war dragged on for another twelve years.

It was at this time that the castle keep was built. At first it was a square tower on top of a vast earth mound. Later the earth mound was itself encased in masonry and castle buildings erected within a curtain wall. Then a rich medieval palace was added, and the keep became a place of retreat in times of war or siege. (It was occupied by the French in the post-Magna Carta war of 1216). In less troubled times it was famous for its hunting park, in the days when the bishop had a large retinue and lived in princely style, often entertaining the king. In the 15th century the palace was embellished with a great entry tower in brick; apparently this was less a fortification than a fashion statement - much as one might add a Victorian-style conservatory to a modern house.

The bishop was lord of the manor of Farnham, and remained so until recent times; with the aid of a royal charter he owned and ruled the town below. The charter seems to have been more a burden than a benefit, and expired in 1790. A guide-book written in 1900 says that in contrast to this lordly past, "Farnham is now ruled by an Urban District Council."

But at least in the 19th century the bishop was still a great local figure. George Sturt, a humble local chronicler, writing in the 1860s, sees him riding in his carriage on his way to church, with two footmen in yellow stockings standing up behind. He still had temporal responsibilities - a conduit carried water from the castle to the lower town, and where water was drawn from a basin there, the door protecting it had the device of a mitre upon it.

This was in the time of Bishop Sumner; when he died, the shops closed and all the men of the town solemnly followed the coffin in procession. The famous Samuel Wilberforce was promoted from Oxford to Winchester, but did not live long enough to occupy Farnham. (We saw how he died in a riding accident at Abinger)

But the great See of Winchester was divided in 1927, and Farnham became the palace of the Bishops of Guildford. The modern, cash-strapped Church of England tried to run the palace as a centre for retreats, but gave up and sold it in 1955. It is now devoted to mammon rather than God, as a thriving and no doubt well-preserved conference centre, but only the castle keep is open to the public.

Of course, Farnham's other famous son is William Cobbett, radical writer and stirrer-up. As a foil to the great establishment figure of the bishop, he was born at the bottom end of town, and his birthplace is suitably the public house that now bears his name.

FRENSHAM

Witch's cauldron

Here is a real legend - that is to say, a story has grown up which nobody can really regard as history, but which has been repeated as long as people can remember. The best one can do is to take a version of it. So here is the story of Mother Ludlam's cauldron, taken from a "Guide to Surrey" written in the 1860s.

Frensham parish church - Mother Ludlams cauldron

"Frensham church is a large stone building, erected in the year 1239 and dedicated to the Virgin Mary. In the vestry is preserved a curious cauldron - a three-legged pot - which seems a curious adornment for the room in which it is placed; but concerning which a tradition is of course current to this effect: near Moor Park is a cavern, which a few centuries ago was known in the locality as Mother Ludlam's cave, it being generally believed that a witch, though certainly a very kind one, made it her abode. Nobody had ever seen Mother Ludlam; but the folks of all the villages around were familiar with her power, which she did not exercise to cause murrain among the cows, or change babies in the cradle, or nip up old joints with rheumatism, after the fashion of witches generally; but to lend cooking utensils and other necessary articles to such poor people as stood in need of them.

"If a ploughman's wife wanted a new pot to boil the children's porridge in, she went to Mother Ludlam's cave at midnight, stated her want, and sure enough it would be ready to put on the fire in the morning. Punctuality in returning the article, however, was insisted on; and one woman having borrowed a big three-legged pot, and thinking she might keep it and Mother Ludlam be never the worse, found out her mistake, for nothing else could ever be obtained, ask as much as anyone would. Nobody liked to have anything to do with the cauldron, for fear it should some day fly up the chimney with the family dinner in it, or that the savoury mess might turn out to be witch broth after all; so it was confided for safe keeping to the clergy of the parish, and was placed in the vestry, where it has behaved itself exceedingly well ever since."

John Aubrey's account (he collected such tales in the seventeenth century) gives a few useful extra details. He describes a stone, to which petitioners would go. "They went to this Stone, and knocked at it, and declared that they would borrow, and when they would repay, and a Voice would answer when they should come, and that they should find what they desired to borrow at that Stone. This caldron, with the trivet, was borrowed here after the manner aforesaid, but not returned according to promise, and though the caldron was afterwards carried to the stone, it could not be received, and ever since that time no borrowing there..."

More sceptical historians think that the vessel once belonged to the great abbey at Waverley, not far away, or it was a typical vessel used in "church ales" and other local feasts of the middle ages. The cauldron is now described, very straightfaced, by the present church guidebook as "a large copper vessel, on an iron trivet, of unknown origin." It is still in the church.

GATTON

Overloaded church

The small church at Gatton, near Merstham, is inside the park, where a great house stood, enriched in the nineteenth century by Lord Monson with costly pictures and decoration. Lord Monson's enthusiasm encompassed his church as well, and he fitted it out with precious pieces of furniture and works of art . The local historian Charles Cox, writing at the beginning of the century, is caustic:

"Every kind of embellishment was introduced, none of which quite harmonizes with its fellows - quire stalls from Belgium, a pulpit from Nuremberg, stained glass from an old conventual church near Louvain, altar-rails from Tongres, and other details from Ghent, Rouen and different parts of Burgundy. The result is a museum-like display, each good of its kind, but hopelessly vulgar in their extravagant rearrangement, and absolutely unsuitable for God's worship in an English village church. The antiquary may succeed in finding an early 13th century piscina niche and font - a pleasant relief from all this exuberance of Continental art."

Gatton parish church - filled with treasures from continental Europe

Visitors can judge for themselves; the exterior looks poor and neglected, in contrast to the richness within. This is arranged like an Oxford college chapel - with stalls facing each other on each side.

GODSTONE

Did you know Surrey was a mining county?

Few activities for which Surrey was noteworthy seem to have left so little trace. For the chalk downs and the greensand ridge have both been honeycombed with mines. Beneath those grassy slopes are passages and caverns galore.

Some that have been best described lie under the North Downs at Merstham and between Godstone and Caterham. Tell-tale signs are place-names : Quarry Hall, Quarry Road - but not as we mostly now find quarries, which are these days open-cast. Clearly, large areas of Surrey are still quarried open-cast, for sand, chalk and fullers' earth. Rather like the coal-mining industry elsewhere in England, stone and sand quarrying was once a business of deep-mining, but the economics of the business and the coming of earth-moving machinery have changed things -scenically at least - for the worse.

Primitive mining may well go back many hundreds of years, but by the year 1600 there were several well-developed sets of workings beneath the chalk downs where the modern A22 runs between Caterham and Godstone. For example, the Arch Cave, started about that time contains miles of passages, covering an extent at least one mile by half a mile, and containing galleries and caverns of enormous size - as big as 400 feet long and 20 feet wide. The prized material was a stone useful for all kinds of building, from sea-docks to furnace linings. It is described as a calcareous sandstone - laid down among the same horizontal strata that produced also the chalk and the sand. This has the great virtue of being reasonably soft to cut, but hardening after exposure to air. Thus it lent itself to deep mining, and could be got by people with no more than hammers and wedges for tools, rather than explosives. It could also be found as it were in complete slabs as it sat in horizontal layers between layers of soft sand.

In this way passages would be cut into almost ready-made square blocks, with the small amount of unusable rubble stored in a previously-cut passage. The product was hauled to the surface up a gradual slope, with no spoil heaps outside to show where the workings were. Advantage was taken of the slope of the downs to get in without having to dig too deep - a sideways attack was made. No doubt there were places at which the different strata could be seen, and efforts would be made to avoid tunnelling through a lot of chalk, which is what lies above.

The early horse-drawn railway that ran to Merstham was used to haul stone towards London, sometimes being transferred to barges at Croydon for shipment by canal to the Surrey docks. Traces of that line can still be seen north of Merstham, and there were mines not far from the Joliffe Arms on the A23. It is near here that there was a tenement for the miners - and some likely-looking foundations could until recently be seen. It is remarkable how few relics of any mining community can be seen, or even recollected.

But the Godstone mines were active until the second world war in 1939, and were then inspected as possible safe storage places. Splendid tales are told of barrels of brandy being stored, but somehow not all the contents remaining as safe as anticipated... Before the war, mushrooms were grown in some of the miles of galleries.

But now the caves are empty and sealed up. The local caving societies have the details and the knowledge - but they also say that "every schoolboy knows" - at least in Godstone - where the hidden entrances are, and that it is impossible to stop this exploration going on. Better, say the cavers, to inculcate some good sense into young people so they take the necessary basic precautions in going underground. And just a word of caution to us all. Both the A22 above Godstone and the M25 at Merstham are built over this honeycomb of caves. Drive carefully!

Perennial rambler

"Minute and Carefully-Prepared Directions for Out-of-the Way Rambles within easy reach of London". This is the heading for an edition ("seventh series") of the Field-Path Rambles of Walker Miles, published in 1894, and price sixpence.

Even in an age when most ordinary folk walked from necessity, many who had the leisure walked for pleasure - increasingly to enjoy unspoiled nature in an escape from sooty London. With the coming of the railways, it became easy to take the train to one station and walk to any number of other small stations through Surrey woods and fields. Obliging railway companies set out cheap fares for groups "friendly and other societies, workmen's excursions".

Walker Miles, the pseudonym of Edmund Seyfang Taylor (1853 - 1908) responded to the need for routes that walkers could take . His little booklets (measuring about 5" by 4") contained closely-packed texts, backed up by notes and alternative routes for substantial walks of about ten to fourteen miles. They indicate -indeed "minutely" - the path to be taken, so they are meant to do away with the necessity of a map.

Godstone churchyard - memorial to Edmund Taylor (Walker Miles)

(However, experience shows that as soon as you misread the way and are lost, such directions are useless without a map) Further instructions are given:

"It is suggested that when a party of several persons set out upon one of these walks, one only of the party should undertake the duty of following out the route, say for a couple of miles or so, and then another take it up; otherwise an engrossing subject of conversation may lead to a path being missed, or a wrong turning being taken."

It must have been not just an obsession - so many walks, such detailed directions - but also a family business.The booklets are published by R E Taylor & Son in the City, who also sell a "Rambler's Companion" - a wallet to contain the booklet, a set of maps, a compass, a box of matches and a note-book - for twelve shillings. Furthermore, a Mrs E S Taylor is the proprietress of the Willow House Tea Rooms in Godstone, advertised inside the back cover ("Rambling Parties Specially Catered For"). Just in case your entertainment is incomplete, another advertisement for "Jog-Trot Rhymes" (price two shillings and sixpence) "suitable for recitation"of which there is a small quotation:

> "If you'ld like a jog-trot ramble through the fields and over stiles
> I'll ask you just to foot with me this baker's dozen miles."

A glance through the booklets shows that thanks to a firm Green-Belt planning policy, many of these walks still exist. Towns and villages have been enlarged, roads widened and metalled, but the field-paths remain and much of the scenery is unspoiled. Some pubs have disappeared, other renamed, but many are recog-

His drawing of turn-of-the-century Merstham

nisable as welcome stops on the way. But it is difficult now to imagine the emptiness and quiet of the late nineteenth-century roads.

Of Burford Bridge , below Box Hill, he writes "This is a charming resort, beloved alike by the modest pedestrian or cyclist, as well as by those who come down from London in style on a four-in-hand."

His accounts, however, usually confine themselves to the route and there is all too little comment on what is being seen. Occasionally he relaxes, if a little oddly:

"Redhill-junction is a convenient station from which to start a ramble; and an important station as well, for trains either of the Brighton Co., or the South-Eastern Co., are on the move to the north, south, east or west, all day long. Therefore, the rambler who upon the termination of his excursion may have half an hour to wait will find incidents of railway life in plenty to engage his attention and while away the time. It is always amusing, if somewhat selfish, when you have plenty of time yourself, to watch the hurry and bustle and excitement and vexation, and often stupidity of other folks who are not so well off in that respect."

Perhaps he lived in Godstone (where Mrs Taylor's tea-rooms were), because he is buried in the churchyard. Fittingly, it is a churchyard through which runs a public foot-path. A nameless rough stone commemorates him, and beside it is a weathered plaque with this verse, in the style, almost of one of his "jog-trot rhymes":

> "This is the bourne to which the footpath led
> This is the spot uncharted in his works
> Twas come upon so suddenly;
> But ever will remembered be
> As where he takes his peaceful rest."

GREAT BOOKHAM

John Aubrey again:

"Near this place is Little Bookeham wherein nothing occurs worthy Notice"

GUILDFORD

The old canal

Just imagine a waterway carrying ships from London to Portsmouth through the leafy Surrey and Sussex countryside!

But this was the vision of entrepreneurs and engineers of the early nine-

Guildford : an old drawing of the Castle

teenth century, spurred on by the problems of war against Napoleon. To replace the doubly hazardous passage of the English Channel and Straits of Dover - subject to both storm and enemy - what attraction there must have been, after a long period of successful canal-building in England, to have a direct link from the Thames to the south coast.

In those days canals (or rivers) were also the best means of moving heavy goods. In Wealden Surrey roads were often impassable except for a few summer months. Loads of timber would be dumped for the winter where they had got stuck fast. Canal transport contributed to the success of the industrial revolution. In Surrey, remote from seaports, building material and especially coal were expensive.

A number of routes from the Thames to the south coast were canvassed and their expense and engineering difficulty assessed. One indeed proposed to use the Coulsdon-Merstham gap through the North Downs, a route already followed by the horse-drawn railway (known as the

Croydon, Merstham and Godstone Railway). The canal would then begin with an inclined plane taking it up to Nutfield, thence via Outwood to Three Bridges and Horsham, and so eventually to join the River Arun and so to the sea. A branch was suggested via Limpsfield to the Medway.

A much less ambitious but still demanding route was eventually adopted, and in 1813 an Act of Parliament was passed for a canal to link the River Wey and the River Arun. Both rivers were already being improved for traffic, but to link them would require 23 locks, mostly in Surrey, of which 8 were close together in Sidney Wood on the Sussex border. A reservoir had to be made near Cranleigh to keep the water in the upper part of the canal topped up.

The canal was opened in September 1816, with horse-drawn barges and occasionally sailing barges - but the canal was too narrow and shallow for large boats. It was never, alas, a paying concern. Like Concorde or the Channel Tunnel, the technology was splendid in principle, but did not pay. All too soon competition with the railways spelt its demise. It did lower the cost of coal - in Guildford the price of coal fell from 3 guineas to 50 shillings a chaldron*

The railway came to Guildford in 1844. After a few years of busy trade in the 1830s, the canal declined. Another Act of Parliament had to be passed to allow it to die (in 1868). But that was not the end. A preservation society is now busy getting the locks rebuilt and the canal bed dredged, its bridges repaired or reconstructed. Footpaths through Sidney Wood near Cranleigh can help you to explore its hilliest bits and see the old lock houses. Further south in Sussex, it can be seen at the crossing of the road from Wisborough Green to Pulborough.

And of course the canalised bit of the Wey can be followed on either side of Guildford, where some of the original barge wharves are preserved.

* *If a chaldron was 36 bushels, work that one out in pounds sterling and kilograms!*

French army invades

When King John reluctantly put his seal to Magna Carta at Runnymede it is said that he was merely buying time. (Perhaps, like modern politicians, king and barons were only displaying gesture politics; perhaps neither side really believed this to be a great day for law and freedom, but each was using it in the hope of getting the upper hand.) Surrey, in these turbulent years, has a brief part of importance in our national story.

Magna Carta solved nothing in the short term. Full-scale civil war broke out, and the rebel barons sent for Louis, Dauphin of France as a rival king. A French army landed at Dover, marched through Surrey and captured the castles of Reigate, Guildford and Farnham. It is difficult now to imagine through how much of the early middle ages England was consumed with rebellion. John was busy further north, losing his baggage in the Wash (as we all know) and dying soon after. Meanwhile the French entered London. But the supporters of the child Henry, who succeeded John, gained the upper hand and the French withdrew the following year, 1217.

A Prodigy Foreseen

John Aubrey, 17th century gatherer of tall tales, must have relished this one from Guildford, concerning the origins of George Abbot, Archbishop of Canterbury, and founder of the Hospital that bears his name:

"His father was a cloathworker and he was born at the first House over the Bridge in St Nicholas' Parish (now - [1692] - a publick House, known by the sign of the Three Mariners) and his Mother when she was with Child of him, dream't that if she could eat a Jack or Pike, her Son in her Womb would be a great Man; upon this she was indefatigable to satisfy her longing, as well as her Dream; she first enquir'd out for this fish but accidentally some of the River water (that runs close by her House) in a Pail, she took up the much desired Banquet, dress'd and devoured it almost all: This odd affair made no small Noise in the neighbourhood and the Curiosity of it made several people of Quality offer themselves to be

Sponsors at the Baptismal Fount when she was deliver'd; this their poverty accepted joyfully, and three were chosen, who maintained him at school, and at the university afterwards."

This was in 1562. It shows how entry to the Church gave opportunities for the poor - if gifted, and more crucially, sponsored - to rise in State and society. Abbot, becoming Dean of Winchester and Vice-Chancellor of Oxford, took a puritan line in opposition to the high church Archbishop Laud. He became Archbishop of Canterbury in 1611, and he opposed King James' "declaration of sports" permitting Sunday afternoon amusements, and was mostly out of favour in the reign of Charles that followed, living in retirement until 1633. A further shadow was cast over his life after he accidentally killed a keeper while hunting in Bramhill Park, Hampshire, but was pardoned by the king in 1621. It was said that bishops were reluctant to be consecrated by a man with blood on his hands.

HOLMBURY ST MARY

Rooms with views

"The woods had opened to leave space for a sloping triangular meadow. Pretty cottages lined it on two sides, and the upper and third side was occupied by a new stone church, expensively simple, with a charming shingled spire."

"..Other houses were built on the brow of that steep southern slope, and others again among the pine trees behind, and northward on the chalk barrier of the downs."

Here, in E M Forster's novel "A Room with a View" (since, as they say, made into a successful movie) are precise descriptions of the Surrey village of Holmbury St Mary. You can visit the expensively simple church, and walk along the road that leads south-west along the brow of

Holmbury St Mary : the expensively simple church of A Room with a View

the greensand ridge towards the ancient camp of Holmbury Hill. Along this road, with steep gardens and tremendous views over the weald into Sussex, are a string of Victorian grand houses - rooms with views indeed. Annoyingly, the film of Forster's novel went elsewhere for its English rural scenes.

The name Holmbury St Mary is synthetic - it unites the little hamlets of Felday and Pitland Street, and dignifies a Victorian development. The story is told (for example, in the leaflet available in the church) of the architect George Edmund Street (perhaps best known for the Law Courts, in the Strand, London) travelling with his wife to Aldermoor - a house on the slope with a view - and Mrs Street saying "It is heaven's gate!" Whereupon Street set about building a house there - and it is the first one along the south-west road - Holmdale. The church - of St Mary - was built in 1879, and the ecclesiastical parish came into existence, giving a new name to the village. Street built the church - at his own expense - partly as a memorial to two wives, both of whom died in the 1870s.

It is clear that Forster must have known the area well - he often stayed with an aunt at Abinger - in a house that he himself eventually came to live in in the 1920s. The church that he describes in a telling phrase as "expensively simple" built of local stone, fits snugly into the hillside. It contains several treasures to suit the high-church taste of Street, notably a della Robbia terracotta of the Virgin and Child. The architectural historian Nikolaus Pevsner, however, is dismissive : "simultaneously extreme care over detail and extreme professional competence in composition and massing, and complete lack of anything to say, the perfect example of form without content."

Anyway, the view from the church porch over the little valley is delightful, and somewhere down there is the muddy lake in which Forster pictures his hero George , the heroine's brother Freddy, and the vicar all going for an impromptu bathe. Forster enjoyed writing that bit.

HORLEY

Pagan shrine

Tucked away in the flat countryside where the Burstow Stream flows towards the River Mole near Horley is the strange mound known as Thundersfield. It is approachable only along narrow tracks from the Smallfield Road or the Balcombe Road. On old maps it is sometimes described as Thundersfield Castle - perhaps at some point in its long history it may have been used as strong point.

For this is a very old site indeed, and historians now identify it with some confidence even if not with complete certainty as a likely Anglo-Saxon pre-Christian shrine. If so, it is a rare place - little record of pagan Saxon times remains. The devout monks who wrote the Anglo-Saxon Chronicle did not care to speak of their pagan predecessors. If there was a shrine here, it was in very thickly wooded, watery country.

KENLEY

Front Line of the Battle of Britain

In a corner of the North Downs, on common land originally owned by the City Corporation of London, is the remains of an airfield, which ought to be as famous as Biggin Hill in Kent. It played a key role in the Battle of Britain in 1940. Without the men and women at such places, invasion might well have taken place and the war have been lost.

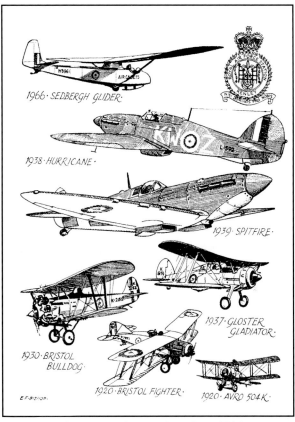

Kenley : aircraft seen there from 1920 to 1966, including the Hurricane and Spitfire used in the Battle of Britain, 1940.

In the last few years the developers have moved in and little remains except the gliding club, and a few derelict barrack buildings. But the history goes back to 1917, and for much of it I am indebted to the book by the late Peter Flint, "RAF Kenley", (Terence Dalton Ltd., 1985) which has gathered not only the strands of official records, but recollections of local eye-witnesses, and some remarkable photographs.

Kenley was developed towards the end of the first World War as a place of assembly and testing of aircraft, which were then required at the front in France. The fact that the area was used at all was due to an active flying pioneer, Conway Jenkins, who was living at the time in Hillbury Road, Whyteleafe, and knew the flat-topped hills across the valley, part of the extensive common land saved for the nation by the City Corporation of London.

Although it was not far from the more famous aerodrome at Croydon, Kenley continued after 1918, despite the objections of local residents. People and despatches were flown from here to and from the Peace Conference in Versailles, using adapted military aircraft - foreshadowing the establishment of regular civil air routes.

It was a time of airshows and aerobatic displays, at which squadrons from Kenley excelled, and by the 1930s the Empire Air Day was an annual event which also helped to recruit personnel for the Air Force. In 1937 a crowd of 10,000 attended. Kenley airfield was still then bisected by a public road (Hayes Lane) only diverted just before the second World War.

Winston Churchill, who was a constant advocate of the need to build up the Air Force against the Nazi threat, had close associations with Kenley, had himself flying experience, and was Honorary Commodore of the famous 615 Squadron. Kenley had just been extended and improved as war came, and its squadrons equipped with the new Hurricane fighter, succeeding the old slow biplanes, like the Gloster Gladiator. After the fall of France, these squadrons withdrew to defend southern England from the expected invasion.

As the history is now clear, Hitler expected to establish air supremacy over the channel and the channel coast so that invasion forces could land unattacked. His deputy Goering held the view that air power alone could cripple London and bring British defeat. The agenda for both was the wiping out of the defending fighter force. Kenley Aerodrome was one of those singled out for attack, and on Sunday August 18th 1940 the attack came.

One of the great achievements of those commanding the Air Force was the establishment of radar (to pick up advance signals of aircraft over the channel) and of effective telephone links and operations rooms so that the routes of incoming attack could be plotted accurately. The Luftwaffe on this occasion used low-level Dornier aircraft which hedge-hopped at fifty feet or so across the countryside to get under the radar cover. Here the defence relied on its team of trained Observers whose reports on this occasion showed that an attack was heading for Kenley. The skill of German pilots and navigators finding their way across country at low level was remarkable. One of their planes carried a photographer whose low-level pictures have been included in Peter Flint's book. And one of his eye-witnesses on that day, Reg Williams, looked out from the third floor of the St Lawrence Hospital at Caterham Hill, directly "into the cockpit of the leading Dornier of the westerly group, noting the steel-helmeted figure of the pilot at the controls as the beautiful green-camouflaged machine flew up Coulsdon Road before turning with its two associates to line up on the aerodrome."

The fighter squadrons, warned of the attack, were already in the air and engaged the successive waves of bombers. Although the airfield and its buildings were badly damaged, its operations room had been overlooked. But it was then moved to occupy a disused butcher's shop a couple of miles away in Caterham Valley.

The next phase of the battle was the sending of large formations of German bombers against London by daylight, escorted by Messerschmitt fighters as powerful as Hurricanes. One of the latter from Kenley's 615 Squadron is now preserved in the Science Museum in London. Although the supply of fighter aircraft (including the new Spitfire) was now good, the toll of fighter pilots in endless sorties over southern England was near-disastrous. Churchill records that in the short period from mid-August to early September 1940 a quarter of the 1000-strong fighter pilot strength was lost. But the daylight attack was blunted and the invasion postponed.

LEATHERHEAD

Birth controller

Leatherhead should be famous; people should flock there to pay their respects to the woman who in this country was foremost in claiming women's proper sexual rights.

Because at a modest house in Leatherhead, a book was written which was a world influence in the twentieth century along with Marx and Freud. Yet this book is no longer in print, and the author little known among the younger generation.

The house was called "Craigvara", the book was "Married Love" and the author Marie Stopes, campaigner for women to know about sex and control their own pregnancies. For a book which no-one wanted to publish, that newspapers would not advertise or review, that booksellers refused to stock, it had an incredible success. It was written in the first world war and published in March 1918. By 1923 it had sold over 400,000 copies and its follow-up, "Wise Parenthood" over 300,000 copies. It would be an understatement to say it provoked controversy - it provoked shock, horror and abuse. All this helped to sell more copies. The book made the shocking revelation of how the sex act took place between men and women, and dared to make the case that women should (and could) have pleasure in sex.

If it was remarkable that such a book should be written, it was just as strange that the author, though she had been married, was still a virgin at the age of 37. After a difficult childhood - but with the asset of an academically-minded mother - Marie blossomed as an undergraduate at University College, London, where she gained a first in botany and went on to postgraduate research. She was awarded a doctorate in Munich and then in London - by which time she was only 25. In 1911 she married a Canadian botanist, but she had this marriage nullified in 1916 on the grounds of non-consummation. In the process she had to read all she could both on marriage law and on the arcane subject of sex. Fortunately for her, she was in a position to read the obscure German texts on this subject locked away in the British Museum. Full now of frustration but also of knowledge she set to to write a book to tell women - and indeed men - how to go about making love and having babies. She also began to campaign to allow women not to have babies they didn't want. The book was written in romantic prose, but did not hesitate to call a penis a penis.

Her enormous energy had already led her to write on many subjects and to meet other writers and famous people; when she was not in Leatherhead she was researching the nature of coal, vital to the war effort. So she was well able to generate publicity by writing to newspapers and to people of influence; she particularly revelled in attacking the Roman Catholic Church, which was not slow to condemn her work. A libel action completed her formation as a national - and then international - figure of notoriety. She became the instant agony aunt of the nation on sex.

The year she published "Married Love" she also married again. This time it was a rich, handsome industrialist also interested in the starting of birth control clinics. The marriage was at first idyllic, and they made their home in another house in Leatherhead - Givons Grove - now demolished and replaced by other houses. Harry Roe was the brother of A V Roe, a famous aircraft manufacturer. They had a son, the object of Marie's every attention, and they together financed birth control clinics across the country, showing mothers how to limit their families by contraception.

As the years passed, the forceful qualities that had created Marie's success proved also to lead to a dictatorial attitude which alienated her fellow-campaigners, her husband and her son. She tried to prevent the latter's marriage to Mary, the daughter of Barnes Wallis the inventor, who also lived nearby. After they had moved to the ultimate house in (or near) Leatherhead in 1933 - Norbury Park, her husband was rarely allowed to live there. Norbury Park is a grand late-eighteenth-century mansion standing in grounds overlooking the River Mole between Dorking and Leatherhead, and facing Box Hill. Much of the grounds are now owned by Surrey County Council and open to the public.

But in this grand setting Marie's influence declined. She still wrote copiously - novels, poems and plays, as well as on human relations and birth control. Her stance was in many ways that of conventional morality - she wrote about sex within marriage - and she also shared the views of many of her time in favouring "eugenics" - the breeding by the best physical specimens, and the discouragment of breeding by the physically inferior.

Although she may have become an impossible wife, mother and colleague, this does not dim her first achievement of writing and getting before the public a book of liberation for men and women, and for starting, in the teeth of all kinds of opposition, clinics to give advice, particularly to the poor, which have been an example ever since. It is hard for us now to understand the virtually universal establishment opposition to contraception, or even to advice about sex, in the 1920s. The Lambeth

Leatherhead : a picturesque view
by the wife of the Rev. James Dalloway (c 1800)

Conference of Anglican bishops, meeting in that year, declared its firm opposition to "teaching, which under the name of science or religion, encourages married people in the deliberate cultivation of sexual union as an end in itself". Marie Stopes had, of course, written them a pamphlet putting them straight on the whole matter, which did rather concentrate their thought. But by 1930, Marie had converted the bishops. She lived on until 1958.

Classical vicar (and his artistic wife)

He is a figure straight out of Jane Austen or Thomas Love Peacock - the leisured clergyman filling his letters with Latin quotations, writing books on local history and laying out his garden in the latest fashion. And he is ever respectful to those noble patrons who have presented him with this comfortable living.

The Reverend James Dalloway, born in in 1763, had completed his classical education with foreign travel afforded by the privilege of a chaplain's post with our ambassador to Constantinople. He returned with reluctance to parish duties in England, but was fortunate to be installed as vicar at Leatherhead in 1801. He was busy on massive histories of Sussex, of ancient statuary and of English painting.

He and his wife laid out the large garden of the Leatherhead vicarage with thought and the best contemporary taste. She was an accomplished artist and drew and etched a number of pretty pastoral views of the River Mole and of the church and vicarage. The pictures, together with Mr Dalloway's Latin-laden text, were published in 1821, and happily re-published by Kohler and Coombes of Dorking in a limited edition in 1975, with a helpful introduction by Francis Steer.

Dalloway casts his text - typically for the late 18th century, perhaps rather than his own time - in the form of letters to his friend. Of Leatherhead he says "The name, which is singular, is not repeated in any of the English counties, and has most frequently suggested to minor wits, a pun or a sarcasm". He goes on to explain, rather ponderously, that the town name was once "Leddrede". He goes on to remind us of Leatherhead's fame as the home (and ale-house) of Elinor Rumming (see page 57), suggesting that the poet John Skelton came with others on a day out, so to speak, from the court of Henry VIII at Nonsuch Palace about six miles distant (between Ewell and Cheam). His wife Harriet gives us a picture of the ale-house (the present day "Running Horse") with Elinor's famous name still on it.

After dealing with the history of Leatherhead, he takes us into his garden, of which he is very proud. In the style of his time, there are not just views from the house, though these were fine indeed. You were meant to take a certain route round the garden, meeting a succession of carefully-designed views, and indeed were expected to have certain thoughts or reflections at each stage. Some gardens carried a whole series of inscriptions to prompt the right sentiment. This, carried to excess, writes Mr Dalloway, is by no means to my taste; but at one point "I ventured to mark the sawn stump of a tree projecting from the banks with the single word 'Philosophemur' - Can a more gentle hint be given?" I am sure every reader will agree.

This is a garden where any Jane Austen heroine might cheerfully take a turn, and perhaps even meet a distinguished young man. First the shrubbery is to be admired, with its noble ilex (Dalloway means quercus ilex, the evergreen oak, which would remind him of Italy or Greece). Then via a gravel walk we reach a panorama - the river, a small island, a weir and a prospect of Norbury Park. At this point the visitor should turn and view the vicarage with its recent addition "in the Tuscan style" and then - "I will now lead you to your favourite seat in the sweet-briar walk. Within the narrow compass of a garden, there is seldom room sufficient for distant effects. Minute beauties may abound in a garden of small extent, which should be simple, but not inelegant, above rusticity, yet free from the ostentation of expense. A seat should be of rude or at least plain materials, for it is allowed, that excess in ornament is one of the most obvious errors of false taste."

The circuit continues, descending to the river - "an air of Italian scenery pervades the whole, and I at least fancy myself, to be reminded of some like it, on the north road to Florence." And then there is a grotto - very fashionable - but a modest one (not, as his footnote suggests like the dreadful ostentation at Oatlands Palace at Weybridge, where the Duke of

Newcastle had been said to have spent £10,000!) The garden circuit is completed with a view of a weeping willow and a Lombardy poplar, and so we return to the house.

Alas! little remains of the idyllic garden, and the vicarage, Tuscan

Leatherhead : Elinor Rummin's house (The Running Horse)

addition and all was rebuilt in 1872. But the Dalloways were resigned to change. "The village, much to my regret, is rapidly losing its primary character, and converting itself by a multiplication of inconsiderable houses, into an appendage of the enormous London". And that was written nearly two hundred years ago!

LEATHERHEAD

Loose goings-on in Tudor Leatherhead

"The tunning [ie the brewing] of Elinor Rumming" is a rumbustious - not to say coarse - ballad of Leatherhead at the beginning of the sixteenth century. Elinor Rumming, whose reputation has been preserved by the poet John Skelton, was the lady who kept the "Running Horse" - still there today to have a drink in by the river bridge

References in earlier books on Surrey, when they quote the poem, leave out the more lurid bits , perhaps in deference to the sensitivities of Leatherhead. Skelton starts off with a nice description of the lady herself:

"Droopy and drowsy
Her face all bowsy
Comely cinkled,
Wondrously wrinkled,
Like a roast pig's ear,
Bristled with hair...

"And this comely dame,
I understand, her name
Is Elinor Rumming
At home in her wonning;
And as men say
She dwelt in Surrey
In a certain stead
Beside Leatherhead.."
(...and so on - but then to the beer!)

"She breweth nappy ale
And maketh thereof pot-sale
To travellers, to tinkers,
To sweaters, to swinkers,
And all good ale drinkers,
That will nothing spare
But drink till they stare
And bring themselves bare,
With "Now waya the mare!
And let us slay care."...

(Then the cabaret starts...)

"Thither cometh Kate,
Cisly, and Sare,
With their legs bare,
They run in all haste...
Some wenches come unlaced
Some housewives come unbraced...
Such a rude sort
To Elinor resort
From tide to tide.
"Abide, abide!
And to you shall be told
How her ale is sold
To Maud and to Mold.
Some have no money
That thither come
For their ale to pay
That is a shrewd array!
Elinor sweared, "Nay,
Ye shall not bear away
Mine ale for nought,
By him that me bought!"...
Strike the hogs with a club
They have drunk up my swilling-tub!"

To reinforce the local connection, the composer Vaughan Williams, who lived not far away at Leith Hill and must have known "The Running Horse", set this poem for two soloists, chorus and orchestra in 1936. The music is hectic, breathless and jazzy, as is right for the words. At its first performance, the lady singer noticed the discomfiture of a distinguished lady in the front row of the audience, and offered her smelling-salts. To no avail, as the lady got up and left after the first verse, pronouncing the work "disgusting".

Penny for a corpse

The Reverend S N Sedgwick records (among his Leatherhead legends) a local tradition that the carrying of a dead body can establish a right of way. To prevent this, the owners of The Swan levied a charge of one penny for carrying a corpse through the brewery yard.

LIMPSFIELD

The Limpsfield ghost

An old guide book to the village can bring the long-standing legend of a village ghost up to its own time - the 1930s. The story centres on New Hall, a building demolished about 1750 because it was "troubled". New Hall was said to have been built by William Gresham of Titsey. He was a rich London merchant and banker - Surrey was always a commuter county! It was built in the late 16th century on the site of a grange that had belonged to the Abbey of Battle. It was partially excavated in 1875 and its dimensions recorded.

Stories of ghostly appearances were told throughout the Victorian period. The coachman of the later house at Titsey (just up the hill from Limpsfield), Mr Duncombe, refused to go along Sandy Lane at night. It is along here that a woman in white is seen. Then William Glosby and his son, coming along this road at night, encounter a presence which nudges up to the boy, but is invisible to his father.

Then as late as 1928, the ghost appears in the same area to two ladies from London, who are unaware of the tradition. They are of more enquiring mind, and summon psychical researchers. But this apparently leads to ghostly reprisal. Green glows and chill feelings are experienced; dogs growl and cower. "Ghostly influence gradually spread as far as Blue House Lane". However, by 1931 all manifestations are said to have ceased.

A suitable origin is ascribed to the Limpsfield ghost. She was a beautiful girl seduced by a monk of the priory that was once in the vicinity. Deserted, she committed suicide.

The cellist and the nightingale

This is now a famous story - the stuff of legend, but splendidly true. The bit people know best has been revived in a BBC "docu-drama" not long ago: a young girl takes her beloved cello into the wood beyond her garden and plays on a soft spring night - and the nightingale joins in. The fledgling BBC comes and broadcasts the combined music to a rapturous public. This happened in Surrey in 1924.

To begin at the beginning. The Harrison sisters were all musical - four of them, urged on and educated by their mama. May was a singer, Beatrice a cellist, Margaret a violinist, Monica also a singer. The first three had international concert careers. They wanted a cottage somewhere, and in driving about the Surrey countryside happened upon one for sale, south of Oxted, Foyle Riding.

Through their concert performances they had already become friends with Elgar and Delius, to say nothing of Princess Victoria, a daughter of Edward VII. Once established in their cottage - which was immediately enlarged, and the adjoining barn turned into a music room - they gave musical parties for important guests. But Beatrice also stole out into the woods, and listened to the nightingale who seemed to respond to her playing.

Her contacts with the BBC, arising from broadcast concerts, led her to suggest that others might like to share the magical sound of nightingale accompanying cello. In May 1924, with all the heavy paraphernalia of early wireless technology, it happened! A broadcast concert was interrupted to make way for the nightingales at 10.45 pm - live of course, - and history was made. And repeated a week later, even more successfully, according to Beatrice.

The Harrison family, for all their grand connections, were eager to share not only the broadcast but the direct experience with a wider public. For a number of years there were "Nightingale Festivals" in which the public were invited - for a modest shilling - to enjoy the gardens and the nightingales from afternoon till dawn. "Buses will meet all trains from Oxted station".

Foyle Riding, its barn and bluebell woods are still there - each a separate and opulent residence these days. The Harrisons left in 1939, after the death of both parents, and with May living mostly in London. But their next home was not far away - and even more venerable - Woolborough Farm in Outwood. Here they spent the war - still active in music. Treasured possessions were destroyed when a V1 (flying bomb) landed on an outhouse, but luckily the house and its occupants were unharmed. That same year, 1944, saw the death of their father's brother, who lived with them. Local papers record his funeral, with full military honours, at Outwood church.

Beatrice died in 1965, but her sister Margaret lived on until 1995 in the same neighbourhood. We have another glimpse of Beatrice playing her cello in the wartime film "Demi-Paradise", a kind of gentle propaganda film starring the young Laurence Olivier. She comes in as a vignette of British values, having already become part of a living national legend.

Musicians at rest

Beatrice Harrison again - and her family - are largely responsible for the fame of Limpsfield churchyard.

St Peter's, parish church of the pretty village of Limpsfield, is well worth a visit in its own right. But its churchyard is surely unusual as the last resting place of musicians. Here are three Harrison sisters - Beatrice, Monica and May. But it must be because of their friendship that Frederick Delius is buried here. He spent his last painful years in France, but used to visit the Harrisons, who had given first performances of some of his work. His wife is buried here too.

Limpsfield : graves of
famous musicians:
Frederick Delius
(1862 - 1934)

Sir Thomas Beecham (1879 - 1961)
and pianist Eileen Joyce (died-1991)

But here also is another famous Delius champion - Sir Thomas Beecham, and the Australian pianist, very famous in the post-1945 period, Eileen Joyce. And more recently, the conductor Norman del Mar.

LIMPSFIELD CHART

Writers and Readers

At the end of the last century Limpsfield Chart, remote in its woods, became the unlikely home for a number of famous writers, including Joseph Conrad, Ford Madox Hueffer and the literary couple Edward and Constance Garnett.

Interestingly, it preserves a village reading-room, where those unable to read could have their letters read to them - for a fee.

LINGFIELD

Enclosing the common land

Large areas of Surrey were until well on in the nineteenth century uncultivated heathland, used as commons. Usually they were owned by

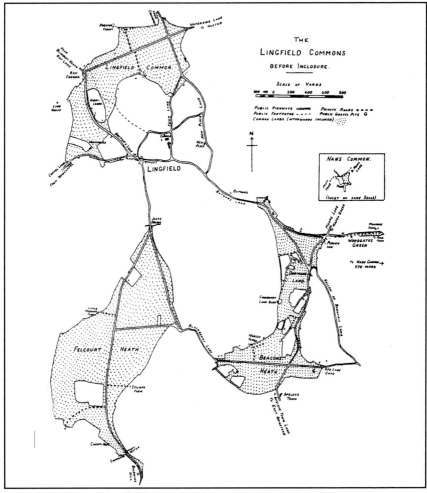

*Lingfield - a map of the commons before the
enclosures of the early 19th century*

the local lord of the manor, but local people had rights to graze animals and to collect firewood. As a result, the landscape looked much more open than it does now - both because there were fewer hedged fields and because tree growth was prevented by grazing animals. Minor roads were muddy or dusty tracks that wound across the open land between enclosed farms; often these were broad "green lanes" with wide verges and strips of woodland. For heavy transport purposes such tracks were poor, and frequently impassable in winter.

Although enclosures of such land had been proceeding for centuries, and sometimes had a bad reputation as a confiscation of peasants' rights, the enclosures of the nineteenth century often had local support. They had the effect of making new land available in small plots for cultivation or building, and of paying for new roads to improve communications.

One example is recorded in Lingfield parish, in the very east of the county, where heath land would seem less obvious. Nonetheless (records a parish guide printed in the 1930s) out of over 9000 acres in the parish, 660 were common land - principally Lingfield Common to the north of the village (the road still bears the name), Felcourt Heath in the south - now much built over - and Dormans Land and Beacon Heath in the south east of the parish.

In accordance with the Act of Parliament, in July 1809 commissioners were appointed who did not have a local interest, and they first arranged a survey to measure the land concerned. The maps so produced (as in this case) are usually preserved in parish records. In October the first sale was held of plots of land, and sales proceeded until the process was completed at a public meeting held in Godstone in 1816. In the interim plots of all sizes were sold, many being less than 5 acres. Most of the money raised was used to construct new parish roads - and these are the boringly straight roads often encountered in this part of Surrey. The wide track of the old road is narrowed, and the old verges absorbed into the fields on either side. In some parts of Surrey - roads round the village of Outwood are a good example - the earlier road lines are marked by old oaks, now standing in lines well back from present-day hedges.

Some of the land was not sold, but allotted to commoners in exchange for their common rights, now extinguished. In the case of Lingfield, this amounted to 77 acres.

Miniature cathedral close

Guildford may have its stark modern cathedral, but Surrey has few major medieval churches of any size. No wool-based prosperity that raised great churches in East Anglia or the Cotswolds. But tucked away in the eastern corner of Surrey is a church in a setting like a cathedral in miniature. It has all the right accessories - a tranquil "close" with timbered old buildings, fine medieval brasses, misericords, lectern. By Surrey standards it is a large church, with what looks like a double nave.

Above all, it has two splendid tombs with the effigies of their occupants lying grandly on top of them. They are both of the Cobham family, once great hereabouts, and the younger of whom (Sir Reginald) was responsible for the rebuilding of the church in the fifteenth century. He

Lingfield - the way into the Close

founded a College - a small community of priests and clerks, but not monks. There were also to be "thirteen poor persons" so it was almshouse as well. Of this, little remains, except the fine timber-framed house now housing the public library, and the other building across the green, built out of old materials from the College. The quiet green space and the largely unspoilt group of buildings around the church make this part of Lingfield like a miniature of Salisbury or Chichester. A glance at book illustrations of the beginning of the century shows that, mercifully, little has been altered.

But back to the Cobhams; Sir Reginald lies in full armour, as befits a soldier who fought at Agincourt ; he died in 1436. His grandfather lies in the large north chapel, in the armour of his period. At his feet lies a "soldan" - the turbaned figure of a Saracen, green of face and weary of expression. This Cobham fought at Crecy and died in 1361. Their castle was at Sterborough, a few miles to the east in the flat valley of the River Eden, feeding the Medway. Nothing now remains of it, except a moat and later buildings constructed from some of its stones. But we may imagine a castle like that at Bodiam in Sussex - towering four-square over its watery surroundings and good enough (in the fifteenth century) to keep custody of Cobham's royal prisoner, the Duke of Orleans.

MICKLEHAM

Marrying the enemy

At St Michael's church, Mickleham on the 28th of July 1793 a remarkable wedding took place. The bridegroom was Alexandre Jean-Baptiste Piochard d'Arblay, a refugee from France. Though in desperately reduced circumstances, he had been a general, and claimed the title of Count Piochard d'Arblay.

He was exiled from France where revolutionary terror was raging. Just down the road, at Juniper Hall, a remarkable gathering of the aristocracy of France was living a hand-to-mouth existence, and hearing the awful news of the execution of their king, Louis XVI and his queen, Marie Antoinette. Despite the continual war between England and France, relations between refugees and locals - especially the local gentry - were very cordial. To English country society the foreigners still represented elegance and refinement .

And the bride? In her way, also a most unlikely character. She was 40, and no great beauty, and with little money, but she had already had two remarkable careers. She had had an overnight success as a novelist in 1778 with 'Evelina', the story of an innocent young girl precipitated into the rakeish society of London and avoiding with difficulty the snares of unpleasant and powerful men. After various adventures there is a suitably happy ending in which Evelina is recognised as the heiress of a baronet and marries a lord. Just the kind of long-lost book that does well on television these days. The book had praise from Dr Johnson and was read by all the important people, and its author, Fanny Burney, emerged from anonymity into London literary society. She at last freed herself from the daughterly duties of caring for her father Dr Burney, who was himself a well-known musical scholar.

From her society contacts, a second career beckoned. She was offered a post at court - an assistant to the Queen's Mistress of the Robes, with the apparently glittering prospect of the round of royal engagements and life in a palace with King George III and Queen Charlotte. Her father urged her - and she accepted. But the drawbacks were fearful. For a modest salary she became a domestic slave. She was required to dress the Queen elaborately every morning at seven, and then a few hours later, at mid-day, to dress her again in other robes, and to stand in attendance until she dropped. After a few hours off in the evening, during which her only relaxation was to be required to play endless games of cards with the Mistress of the Robes, she had to undress the Queen at midnight.

Eventually after four years, her health broke. With great difficulty she obtained permission to retire from court, and was granted a pension of £100 a year. She picked up her more agreeable (and better paid) life in literary London, and wrote more novels. With the proceeds of one of these, 'Camilla' she was able to have built a small cottage across the valley from Mickleham, on land leased to her by friends in the big house there, Norbury Park. Indeed, it was while staying there that she had become acquainted with the nearby French colony, and having married, the couple lived an austere, Wordsworth-like existence, cultivating the garden, keeping goats and living on Fanny's pension.

Mickleham - plaque commemorating Fanny Burney and the French emigres of 1792

Then new challenges called. There was a brief lull in the desultory war with France, and the revolutionary terror had subsided. They travelled to France, where General d'Arblay hoped to resume his military career, reclaim his rights and support his wife and their son. But he wanted to stipulate that he would not be required to fight against his wife's country in any future war! However, in a very short time war broke out again: a turbulent decade culminated in the chaos and carnage of Waterloo, in which Fanny and her husband were parted and both their lives were at risk.

They survived - but the rest of Fanny's life was difficult and sad. Her husband died not many years after, and so did her young and brilliant son. Her later books were not well received, and she was obliged to sell Camilla Cottage. Alas, the cottage too, surviving with relics of her occupation until 1919, was burned down, and a modern house stands on its site. She herself lived until 1840, devoting herself to publishing the journals and letters of her musical father, which give us an insight into the world of the time of Mozart. But literary critics were scathing about her prose style, which retained the heaviness and complication that perhaps she had learned from Dr Johnson. By the time she died in 1840 the new age of Victoria was a long way from the world of George the Third.

OAKWOOD HILL

Chapel in the Clearing

"There is nothing of interest in the hamlet of Oakwood Hill, except one or two picturesque cottages and a roadside tavern", says Ogilvy, whose massive two-volume work on Surrey, illustrated with his own paintings, appeared in 1914. But as he goes on to say, "quite huddled in the woods and only to be reached from the village by field-paths is Oakwood chapel".

Oakwood Hill - the church in the woods

It is a place to be sought out for its unexpected location. Although restored and added to in the nineteenth century - (what Surrey church escaped, except the abandoned church of Albury? -) its almost magical setting, deep in the woods, speaks to us from the remote past. Surrounded by its tiny churchyard, it seems about to be swallowed up by the trees, and only footpaths lead to it. (It is a short walk from the road on the south side, with its cottages as Ogilvy describes. His "roadside tavern" - The Punchbowl - looks prosperous enough)

As elsewhere in Surrey, where parishes are large tracts of country and going to church can be a long journey, this is a "chapel of ease" - a closer local place of worship to attend than a parish church in Abinger or Ewhurst. After all, in the seventeenth century you could be fined for not attending church. Oakwood Hill has been such a chapel since the thirteenth century, and was little altered until 1879, when it was enlarged to about twice its original size by the addition of a north aisle. At one stage around 1700 it almost fell into ruin, and was repaired by contributions from John Evelyn, who owned much of the land near here.

OCKLEY

The battle of Ockley

This is one of Surrey's earliest appearances in the history books, and even this is disputed. Some historians place Aclea in Hampshire, but there are some compelling pieces of evidence that this great battle to defeat the marauding Danes took place on the edge of the Surrey weald, near the village of Ockley.

The Anglo-Saxon Chronicle has these words:

"And the same year (AD 851) came three hundred and fifty ships to the mouth of the Thames, and stormed Canterbury, and put to flight Beorhtwulf, king of Mercia, with his levies, and went then south over

Ockley - a stretch of the Roman road (Stane Street) which would have been used by Anglo-Saxon and Danish armies

Thames into Surrey; and king Æthulwulf and his son Æthelbald, with the West Saxon levies, fought against them at Acleah, and there made the greatest slaughter of a heathen host that we have ever heard tell of, and there won a victory."

Now some historians tell us that, contrary to the views of other historians, the Romans left their roads behind in fairly good shape, so that these roads were still, in Saxon times, the only practical way of getting about for military purposes. Only the king and his armies - and enemy invaders - had a need to travel far; everyone else had to be content to stay in his village. It is surmised that the Danes, having sacked Canterbury and London, were after Chichester and ships home. Stane Street would take them. Striking through the north downs between Leatherhead and Dorking, the road passes close to the old fort on Anstiebury Hill as it crosses the sand-ridge, before plunging into the forest of Andredsleag. Here the Danes were met and overwhelmed by the Saxon forces. Other accounts add that fugitives from the battle were pursued and destroyed in nearby Gatton, and that songs were sung to commemorate the great battle.

Anyway, considerable human remains were dug up on Etherley Farm, just below Leith Hill, in 1822.

OUTWOOD

Benevolent squire

Mr Alfred Lloyd, the scion of a banking and stockbroking family, bought the estate of Harewoods in the parish of Bletchingley in 1875, and subsequently farms and common land around, becoming lord of the manor of Burstow.

His obituary in 1919 says "he was always looked up to as a kindly landlord, a good friend and neighbour, a stalwart supporter of fox-hunting and a shining example of the fact that foxes and pheasants can both be plentiful in the same coverts where the owner intends they should be."

His son, Theodore, continued the benevolent tradition, which included building and endowing the village hall in Outwood. He had no children, but adopted an orphan nephew as his heir. But somehow they became estranged. There were no near relatives to whom the estate could be left; so that it should remain intact, it was left to the National Trust.

Millers' tales

Visitors to Outwood, once a small hamlet on the edge of nowhere, see the famous post-mill built in 1665, whose sails still turn today. Bright and new painted as it stands today, its long history has been an alternation of prosperity and decay.

The mill was originally in the Budgen family, who in more recent times became well-known as grocers, but passed to the Jupp family, related to the Budgens by marriage, in the early nineteenth century. About that time a second and even larger mill was built, a smock mill with an iron mech-

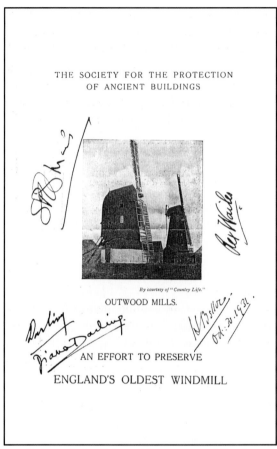

*Outwood - leaflet used for an appeal for the
restoration of the post-mill, 1931 (signatures
include those of Hilaire Belloc and S P B Mais)*

anism. (The post mill, as it name implies, carries wooden machinery supported on one great oak post.) The more colourful version of the story is that two Budgen brothers quarrelled, and one set up a new mill in rivalry to the other, and "to take the wind out of its sails."

It is not clear exactly when the second mill was built. Land for it was granted to William Budgen by the then lord of the manor of Burstow in 1796, on a 200-year lease. Incidentally, although the wording of the lease has been quoted in at least two instances, nobody can now trace the document. The smock mill was certainly operating by 1842, when it appears on a local tithe map. Guide books to Surrey written around 1900 comment on the spectacular sight of the two mills together, standing on their 400-feet-high ridge, with views to north and south - and a view of Leith Hill, now obscured by trees - in this then isolated spot. Roads were then little more than heaps of loose stones - the road to Bletchingley was like that until the second world war.

The mills saw the prosperity (for farmers and millers, anyway) of the Napoleonic wars, and subsequent depression, with bad harvests and competition from imported grain. By 1914 the smock mill ceased to work regularly, and is shown in pictures with only two of its four sails. By the 1930s the post mill had the same appearance, but help was at hand. The Society for the Protection of Ancient Buildings, founded by William Morris, had a section dealing with mills, and they launched an appeal for funds to repair this oldest survivor.

To publicise the appeal they held a special meeting at Outwood, at Harewoods, the home of Theodore Lloyd, then lord of the manor of Burstow, on whose land the mills stood. A leaflet was published by the SPAB to record the event, and to request donations. The Society aimed to raise £90 to provide two new sails and repair the existing ones. "In consideration of this gift, the miller, who holds the mill on a 500 years lease, and Mr Theodore Lloyd, who possesses manorial rights over the mill, have agreed to enter into a Deed of Covenant with the Society, whereby they promise never to demolish the mill, to keep it in repair in accordance with the terms of the lease and to require any future purchaser of the mill to enter into a similar Covenant with the Society. Thus for the cost of a new pair of sails, the safety of Outwood mill will be ensured for future generations."

The meeting was memorable for being attended by the writer Hilaire Belloc (best known these days for his comic verse "Cautionary Tales for Children") who owned a windmill at Shipley in Sussex.

So the money was raised and the covenant signed. However, it took years for the work actually to be carried out, and for the mill to be turning again. But during the second world war, the mill contributed to the war effort by grinding flour under a government scheme, only to fall into disrepair again afterwards. Again the Society for the Protection of Ancient Buildings had to step in to make a public appeal - and in hard and austere times, when few people had the opportunity or transport even to visit a still out-of-the-way place.

In 1954 the mill was ready to turn again. Theodore Lloyd, now an old man, proposed to hold a re-opening ceremony, but there is no evidence that this took place.

The smock mill was less fortunate. In 1944 its owner, Walter Scott, appealed to the SPAB for help, but for the Society it was one mill too many. Their technical experts reported that it would be too expensive - although it was agreed that the combination of the mills was a feature worthy of preservation. Surrey County Council was approached but declined to help. The smock mill collapsed in 1960 and nothing of it remains.

PETERSHAM

Notorious Duchess

Ham House, recently restored to its 17th century splendour by the National Trust, stands near the Thames just above Richmond. In its hey-day it was the centre of political intrigue of the Restoration period, and its mistress, who became Elizabeth, Duchess of Lauderdale, was a larger-than-life character who epitomises the ruthless pursuit of power and wealth of that troubled time.

The house was built in 1610; its exterior is somewhat altered from that date - looking to my view more like an Edwardian boarding school than a stately home. In 1625 it was bought by William Murray, Earl of Dysart, and later was owned by his daughter Elizabeth, who became Countess in her own right. She had married Sir Lionel Tollemache, and descendants of that family were the later owners of Ham House.

By now we are in the turbulent times of the Civil War and the subsequent Commonwealth. The Countess managed to keep in with both sides, being a reputed mistress of Oliver Cromwell and a friend to beleaguered monarchists under threat of death. One of these for whom she successfully pleaded was the Earl of Lauderdale, captured at the battle of Worcester.

There were "love passages" between the two, says a discreet Surrey guide of the 1900s - though both were already married. In due course their unwanted spouses both conveniently died, and the two were free to marry, which they did without delay. With Charles II's restoration they became two of the most powerful people in the kingdom. In 1672 they were created Duke and Duchess of Lauderdale and the Duke was de facto ruler of Scotland on behalf of Charles. "The fury of his behaviour heightened the severity of his ministry, and made it more like the cruelty of the Inquisition than the legality of justice".

As for the Duchess, she was the power behind the throne; she sold the offices of state to the highest bidder, and lavished the proceeds on Ham House. She is spoken of as having a "loose and scurrilous tongue". In a Scottish ballad ("mostly too gross to quote")

"She is Besse of my heart, she was Besse of old Noll;
She was once Fleetwood's Besse, now she's Besse of Atholle;
She's Besse of the Church, and Besse of the State;
She plots with her tail, and her Lord with his pate.
But now she usurps both the sceptre and Crown,
And thinks to destroy with a flap of her gown."

The Duke died in 1682, after years of kidney disease - perhaps not helped by gross overeating. His Duchess survived him until 1698 and was buried in Petersham Church - but there is no monument to her memory.

Ham House is her monument. It benefited from subsequent neglect - it was never remodelled on Georgian or Victorian lines. By 1770 Horace Walpole sees it as old-fashioned - "the old furniture is so magnificently ancient, dreary and decayed" and so it remained. There is a legend that the great gates facing the river were closed when Charles I was executed, and have never been opened since. In the early 1900s the house was described as eerie, melancholy and redolant of the ghosts of the Duke and Duchess. The Tollemache family presented it to the National Trust in 1948; a long period of restoration ensued, culminating in its re-opening in splendour in 1995.

PILGRIMS' WAY

- a Surrey myth

One of the best-known antiquities of Surrey must be the long ridge-way universally known as the Pilgrims' Way. Still on the shelves of the public libraries are copies of old books describing in great detail how "thousands of pilgrims" used to flow from Southampton or Winchester along the chalk downs into Surrey and so along the north downs all the way into Kent and on towards Canterbury. Authors like Hilaire Belloc (1910) and Julia Cartwright (1895) produced handsome illustrated books, identifying all the likely sights and stopping-places the pilgrim traffic would have encountered.

More than that, the Ordnance Survey maps showed inscriptions in olde-English lettering identifying "Pilgrims' Way" at several points in Surrey. Interestingly, present-day OS maps still show the inscription - but in modern lettering.

But today historians agree that the story is untrue. There is no evidence that pilgrims ever went from Winchester to Canterbury, or that they used the trackways of Surrey.

Let us start with the bits that are true. Yes, of course there were pilgrims who went to Canterbury. They went to visit the shrine of St Thomas, murdered in December 1170 and canonised in 1174. Interestingly, to accommodate this traffic, they moved Thomas's remains from the crypt of the cathedral to a new and sumptuous shrine in July 1174, with the convenient result that pilgrims could come in the summer, and not the inhospitable winter. And we have the evidence of Chaucer's famous book "Canterbury Tales" that pilgrims indeed went from London to Canterbury. And perhaps - but only perhaps - the king who unwisely or unwittingly suggested that Thomas be disposed of - Henry II - returning to England from France, travelled through Surrey from Winchester to Canterbury to do penance at the shrine. But then again, historians think he may have gone via London.

The other bit that is true is that there are ancient track-ways along, or just below, the north downs - or sometimes, along the sand ridge immediately parallel to the south. They are thought to go back into the mists of prehistory, but were in regular use, say, in Roman times and after. Here

Pilgrims Way? - a section of the ancient trackway, near Caterham

and there the authentic ancient route is identified by the map-maker. How then did the legend arise?

One of the most interesting accounts - or, indeed two accounts - can be found in the books of Eric Parker, who wrote "Highways and Byways in Surrey" in 1909 and later - in the nineteen-forties - wrote the book on Surrey in the County series. In the second book he explains that his account of forty years before is not true, and tries to uncover how the myth can have come about. He pins the blame on a Victorian cartographer with a taste for colourful history, possibly putting in the conjecture about Henry II. Since then, of course, various country lanes, farms and cottages have attached the name 'pilgrims' to themselves, and the trackway in its several appearances has come to take the customary name of "Pilgrims'

Way". But that is all. The rest of the colourful detail - that Shalford Fair near Guildford was connected with the pilgrimage (and with John Bunyan and "Pilgrim's Progress" for good measure), and that St Catherine's and St Martha's Chapels near Guildford were stops on the route - is mere pleasant fancy.

So for modern walkers, we just have the North Downs Way and a little to the south of it the Greensand Way, traversing the County from west to east. At various points, parts of the Old Road can be seen close by.

REDHILL & REIGATE

The painter and his father-in-law

Samuel Palmer was a notable English painter with a special, almost magical style. Although some of his landscapes are straightforward - though always brilliant and memorable - others are dreamlike and intense. They may be peopled with a shepherd or a sleeping boy, and are very English, but the hills are more enfolding, the valleys deeper, the corn more luxuriant, the moon larger than they have a right to be.

He came to Surrey in his later years after some time at Shoreham just over the Kent border, having been as a young man a disciple of William Blake, from which much of the luminous visionary character of his painting must derive. Born in 1805, his life was a long struggle of the kind we associate with the artist - never gaining the recognition he needed in his own lifetime, but devoted to his own vision and vocation.

Apart from rural England, he did get to see the European artist's great inspiration, Italy. He went there after marrying the daughter of a much more prosperous artist, John Linnell, and returned with sketches and paintings of the great classical views and landscapes. His marriage to Hannah Linnell kept them from complete poverty, but only at the cost of financial dependence on Hannah's father. More than that, Palmer seems to

80

have been intimidated by his father-in-law's dominance, and his married life racked by tension.

Linnell moved to Redhill, to a house called Redstone Wood - somewhere on Redstone Hill, but now demolished - and the Palmers too moved in 1862 to the fresh air and rural views of Surrey. They lived in Furze Hill House, now called The Chantry, which still stands on Cronks Hill at the top of Meadvale in Reigate, with its own magnificent view southward over the Weald (if you ignore Gatwick Airport!).

Late in life he began to receive the recognition due to him, and his paintings and etchings began to sell. Links can be traced between Palmer and the Pre-Raphaelites like Burne-Jones. Both he and his father-in-law painted the Surrey countryside, and both lie buried in Reigate churchyard. Palmer died in 1881 and Linnell the following year.

REIGATE

Temperance Lady

Isabella Caroline, Lady Henry Somerset (1851 - 1921), was the archetype of the Victorian bountiful lady. She was the daughter of an Earl who had married one of the celebrated Pattle sisters, renowned for their beauty and their aristocratic marriages. Another Pattle, Maria, had a daughter who married Leslie Sttephen and was the mother of Virginia Woolf.

But back to Isabella. Like her mother she made a grand marriage, to Lord Henry Somerset, a charming man. Though the Dictionary of National Biography is discreet about it, more recent biographers have been able to be less reticent. As one puts it "Lord Henry preferred the embrace of the second footman to that of his wife." When this eventually became a public scandal he fled to Italy.

On his death in 1883 she inherited the estate which included their home at Reigate Priory. Its mediaeval remains had long been encased in later building, and it shows a modest 18th century facade to its park (now public) and the building itself is now a school, with a small museum open on Wednesday and Saturday afternoons in term-time.

After this unsatisfactory marriage Lady Somerset devoted the rest of her life to the cause of temperance, particularly among women. It is said that she had been profoundly shocked by the suicide of a woman friend through drink. She led the British Women's Temperance Association for many years and was a leading influence also in the World Temperance League, parting from it when American temperance policy pressed for prohibition.

Reigate - the model village at Duxhurst
(Lady Somerset's cottage)

The mark she left on Surrey was in the form of a colony for inebriate women, founded on land at Duxhurst, south of Reigate. Here the women could lead a new life. There were thatched cottages round a village green; a church, a pottery, a laundry and a farm. The village was opened by Princess May (the future Queen Mary) in 1896 and here Lady Somerset took up her abode. As an institution it was said to be the first of its kind, and the inmates were treated not as criminals but with courtesy, trust and sympathy.

Alas, the colony is long derelict. If you take the bridle-path from Crutchfield Lane to the Reigate Road you see a ruined farm, some odd new houses here and there, and just one survivor - Lady Somerset's cottage. As a cottage, though humbly thatched, it is rather grand, and one

82

hopes it is a listed building. But the church and other buildings, and the cottages round the village green, have all been demolished.

The Mystery of the Barons' Cave

A few steps away from an ordinary High Street - up a narrow passageway next to Boots, actually - and you are inside the grounds of the ancient castle of Reigate. Like so many other Surrey relics, there is virtually nothing left of it. Except a large mound - and an underground passage and cave. (To try and make it more romantic, a Mr Barnes in the eighteenth century caused to be erected a fancy gateway in the Gothick style).

But the cave and its passages have no satisfactory explanation. They are now under the benevolent control of the Wealden Cave and Mine Society, who open it to the public and give guided tours on certain days of the year. (Ask the Reigate and Banstead Borough Council)

At the base of the castle mound, down in the dry moat, is a door, and steps lead gently down - all very Enid Blyton. The passageway leads on through the heart of the mound, with a side chamber of irregular shape where sand was dug. It then leads upward, becomes a flight of steps and eventually sees the light of day through a grille at the top of the castle mound, where it is crowned with a little pyramid of stone. So far, so good. Every castle ought to have an escape route, or a secret entrance; the digging of sand (which used to be extensive under the mound, but made the passages unsafe) was everywhere in this part of Surrey. But the distinctive and mysterious part is another passage branching off near the lower entry.

This is wide, high, gently curving (following the line of the circular mound) and ending with a semi-circular stone bench. The arched ceiling is finely smoothed. Here and there, as in the other passage, are initials cut and occasional rough carvings, and dates - the earliest being 1644. It is too grand to be a mere mining tunnel, and almost suggests a meeting place.

The myth grew up, handed on by that romantic writer Martin Tupper, that this was "The Barons' Cave" and here gathered the rebellious (or free-

Reigate - in the caves (Photograph by courtesy of Wealden Cave and Mine Society)

dom-loving, which ever you prefer) nobles of England intent on curbing the power of the wicked King John. Here they drew up Magna Carta. Alas, there is no evidence at all for this, although the castle was in working order then, but probably offered superior accommodation for such plotting above ground.

The name persists, but is nowadays strictly in inverted commas, and the guides will make it clear that the stories are stories only. But we are left with a wide vaulted passage looking for a history.

WARLINGHAM

Woe waters

"In the same yere womere watere ranne hugely, with suche abundaunce of water, that nevyr manne sawe it renne so muche afore this tyme. Womere is callede the woo watere: for Englyschmen, when thei dyd fyrst inhabyd this lond, also sone as thei see this watere renne, thei knewe wele it was a tokene of derthe or of pestylence or of grete batayle; wherefore thei callede it womere, which signyfieth woo watere...[and there is one] at Croydone in Suthsex that when it betokeneth batayle it rennys foule and trouble watere..."   (John Warkworth's Chronicle of 1473)

84

Later, in the seventeenth century John Aubrey comes upon this information:

"A little below in a grove of Ew trees, within the Manor of Westhall in the Parish of Warlingham as I have frequently heard, rises a spring upon the approach of some remarkable alteration in Church or State which runs in direct course between Little Hills to a place called Foxley Hatch and there disappears and there is no more visible till it rises again at the end of Croydon Town near Haling Pound where with great rapidity it rushes into the river near that Church. I must not here forget to observe that Rusticks are obliged to drive their cattle a great Way for water.

It began to run a little before Christmas and ceased about the end of May at that glorious Aera of English liberty the year 1660. In 1665 it preceded the Plague in London and the Revolution of 1688"

Older residents may know that "Foxley Hatch" equates to the cross-roads at Purley, until not long ago described in bus timetables as "Purley Fountain", alas long gone. However, flooding at that point was frequent and annoying up to about the 1970s.

Modern science, of course, soberly tells us that when there is prolonged rainfall, water seeps out of the porous chalk into the otherwise dry valley that runs north from Woldingham to Croydon.

At its greatest length, it has been recorded as a stream seven miles long from Bug Hill Farm, below Warlingham, to the River Wandle in Croydon. However, rivers are not what they were; and it is also not for nothing that the East Surrey Water Company squats athwart the path of the woe water (or Bourne, as it is otherwise known) at Kenley, on the Surrey-Croydon border. But in a really wet winter, the water flows - if only by fits and starts. A good flood was seen as recently as 1988 near the Wapses Lodge roundabout on the A22, between Caterham and Whytleafe.

WAVERLEY

Monastic Miracles

Although all that remains is now a mere vestige, this was once a grand and powerful Cistercian abbey. It has attracted legends in its time, and John Aubrey, diligently gathering these in the seventeenth century, tells us the following:

"In 1210 King John raised so severe a Persecution against the Cistercian Order in general as well as more particularly against this Convent, that he seized their Estate and Goods, and forc'd the Abbot to fly privately away by night to save his life about St Martin's tide and dispers'd the monks. In 1222 the Founder of the new Church was interr'd near the North wall of it. In 1223 a Boy of 7 or 8 Years of Age, standing near the Abbey Gate, fell into the river, on the feast of the Invention of the Cross and by the Rapidity of the Stream was drove through four of the Bridges, and was afterwards found on the Surface of the Water, dead to all outward Appearance, but being taken out and carefully attended, he was brought to life and came to his Post at the Gate from whence he had not been missed nor enquired after".

"In 1228 a Youth fell from the Top of the Tower of this Church and lay for some time stupefied but recover'd without any hurt or pain."

WEST HORSLEY

The Legend of Sir Walter Raleigh's Head

The church of St Mary, with its massive tower, has a chequered history probably going back to Saxon times. Among the many burials there are some of members of the Raleigh family, who for a time lived at West Horsley Place close by.

Sir Walter's son Carew is buried in the south chapel, and "the legend persists" as chroniclers say, that the head of Sir Walter was found buried there too.

Sir Walter, a favourite under Elizabeth, was accused of plotting against her successor, James I. He was released from the Tower to make (at his own expense) a last expedition to find gold in the West Indies. It went disastrously wrong, and Raleigh returned home knowing what his fate would be. It is said that after his execution his widow carried the head about in a red leather bag, and then had it buried beside her son. Sir Walter's body is buried in St Margaret's, Westminster.

WEYBRIDGE

Vanished Palace

The vanished royal palace at Cheam (Nonsuch) is well enough known, but it is not alone in Surrey.

Oatlands Palace was built for Henry VIII but practically nothing except a length of wall and a blocked-up arch - remain. As will be seen from the illustration, it was built on a grand scale. It was abandoned as a ruin in the Civil War,

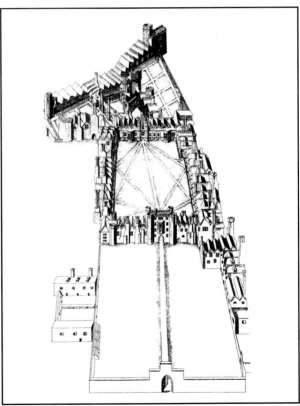

Weybridge - Oatlands Palace, as it was in the 16th century

87

although later houses were built on its site.

Of modern Weybridge my old guide-book says:

"...not a place of special attraction, and it has suffered recently in the eyes of all save professional and semi-professional motorists by its nearness to the Brooklands racecourse, which has destroyed so large a circle of fine woodlands."

In our time, the developer has moved in again: Brooklands becomes a shopping-centre and museum of motor-racing.

The levellers of St George's Hill

There is an irony that the posh part of Weybridge should be overlooked by St George's Hill, with its ancient camp and its story of the Levellers of the Cromwellian period. These splendid Utopian people started what these days would be called a commune of the New Age. Under their leaders Everard and Winstanley they dug and planted on St George's Hill, declaring that all had a right to the land. Cromwell's egalitarianism didn't go that far, and the Levellers were driven off. Here is part of their song:

> You noble Diggers all, stand up now, stand up now,
> You noble Diggers all, stand up now,
> The waste land to maintain, seeing Cavaliers by name
> Your digging does disdain, and persons all defame.
> Stand up now, stand up now.

WITLEY

Painter of cottages

If anyone has immortalised the old Surrey cottage, it is the watercolour artist Helen Allingham (1848 - 1926)- who perhaps did it by accident.

Nineteenth century Surrey was, of course, already a happy-hunting-ground for painters, particularly in Reigate and in the far west of the county. There were plenty of still unspoiled rural views to paint, a ready market among town-dwellers with nostalgia for an imagined rural past, anxious to have something to look at besides the smoke and grime of the city.

Helen Allingham painted cottages because she liked doing it. She had grown up with artistic talent, and needing to earn a living. She had fought for the opportunity to train professionally at a time when women were only beginning to be admitted - grudgingly - to art schools, and joined the book illustration trade. Books and magazines, growing to meet a growing readership, needed a constant supply of illustrators. In this occupation she met William Allingham, a magazine editor, ballad writer and diarist, and married him. Though they can never have been rich, she did not continue book illustration, but turned with relief from black-and-white to colour - watercolour. She sketched and painted the literary friends of her husband - notably Carlyle and Tennyson - and painted rural scenes on their holidays from London.

In 1881 they moved from London to a cottage in Sandhills, near Witley. One reason for the choice was that Tennyson now spent much of the year at Aldworth, close by. William Allingham had always admired Tennyson's poetry and almost attached himself to the Tennysons. Before he could afford to live by literature he took a post at Lymington in Hampshire to be close to Tennyson who then lived at Farringford on the Isle of Wight. The Tennysons tolerated him and he repaid them by leaving detailed diary notes of the great man's sayings and daily doings.

So in the 1880s - with his other great hero, Carlyle, dead, they moved to within walking distance of Aldworth. As a result we have a splendid series of his wife's pictures of cottages particularly in Witley and around. Perhaps a few of these buildings can still be seen today in the West Surrey villages, cleaned up, repaired, sanitised and centrally heated. In Helen Allingham's paintings they are clearly the homes of the poor, at a time of agricultural depression and poverty. For example, there is a "condemned cottage"; there is a description by her husband of a cottage (though not in

Surrey) with a pretty exterior but inside:

"I found a woman, not very old, but worn and wild-looking; toothless, unkempt, no gown on, sitting by a wretched fireplace, of which she began to complain - 'smoke, soot, rain through roof. Agent won't do anything - rent £4, taxes 10s."

And another instance -again, as it happens, in Kent (at Ide Hill) not in Surrey, she is painting an old cottage, and the local doctor remarks that "that house had had more fever in it than any other in the parish." The cottage the

Witley - traditional Surrey building,
as once painted by Helen Allingham

Allinghams took had no water or convenient means of heating; rural gas and electricity were distant prospects. On another occasion the Allinghams and Tennysons go exploring together to find an old cottage they have been told of, that Helen might want to paint.

"A highish field gate was locked, and T. climbed over - then trudging through a swampy field we came to the deserted half-ruinous cottage, with long slope of tiled roof, broken windows and empty barns. H. made a pencil sketch, and T. and I went on further, but could not get through the copse."

Helen usually did all her painting outside: we have the photograph of her well wrapped-up with an umbrella that doubled as easel. By contrast many others (like her Witley contemporary Birket Foster) only sketched outdoors, and did the actual painting in the comfort of the studio.

90

Thanks to her we have a vivid record of Surrey cottages and their cottagers for the 1880s. The Allinghams then returned to London for the education of their children, and soon after, William died.

Fortunately, though such pictures must have gone through a period of unfashionability this century, many survive. A few years ago a fine exhibition of them was seen at the Guildford Borough Art Gallery. Then they appropriately belonged to the Marley Tile Company - there are few paintings that linger so lovingly on the old, often moss-covered, hand-made clay roof-tiles of Old England. Unfortunately, they are now scattered in various ownerships, and Guildford Art Gallery possesses only one.

Fallen Financier's Mysterious Park

Whitaker Wright (1845 - 1904) was a larger-than-life character who made fortunes and lost them. In his youth he went to America, and as a metallurgist was involved in the booming exploitation of the continent's metals. He was at the Leadville mining boom in 1879, then lost a fortune in Philadelphia and came back to England.

He became a Surrey legend a little later in life, after more companies had come and gone. He built Lea House, in what is now called Witley Park, about 1890. He reputedly spent some £840,000 on it, and landscaped the park. The wall enclosing the park was said to have cost £37,000. (You can multiply those figures by 50 or 60 to get today's prices).

The wall is certainly still there, built to keep intruders out. The park's claim to fame is an underwater room, built beneath the lake. It is lit by a glass roof, just below the surface of the lake, thus transmitting an eery light to the interior. Just to add to the effect, a statue of Neptune sits on the roof, so that viewed from the park its base is invisible, and it appears to rise from the lake itself.

The present owners discourage visitors. In one or two guidebooks there are descriptions of the spooky descent from the park down underground passages beneath the lake to the room, described as a ballroom. But a spokeman for the Witley Park estate, refusing my request just to come and look, told me plainly that publicity only encouraged people to try and visit - and "this doesn't fit in with our business as a conference centre."

But back to Whitaker Wright : he created a great finance company, the London and Globe, in 1895, but as a result of his manipulations it crashed and brought down with it investors, both great and small. In the wake of this spectacular fall, Wright was prosecuted for fraud, after being brought back from America, to which he had fled. Sentenced to seven years in jail, he committed suicide, leaving Lea House as his monument. Even this did not survive; after being badly damaged by fire in 1952, it was demolished and replaced with a new house in 1961. The property was renamed Witley Park.

Some earlier guide-books of Surrey are understandably reticent about Whitaker Wright, closer to the scandal and tragedy. Eric Parker, who wrote indefatigably about Surrey until at least 1952, wrote in 1908 "Witley has perhaps been a little overshadowed by the tragedy of a late owner of Lea Park. I have heard descriptions of the new features ... the lakes and fountains and a billiard-room, I believe, under the water, but I have not seen them."

Although a suicide, Whitaker Wright was buried in Witley churchyard.

WOKING

City of the dead

The anonymous writer of a tourist's guide to Surrey in the 1860s describes Woking as a little town with a population of 3819. This is what the maps now call Old Woking, before the railway had done its work in throwing up a new settlement. But already by then the railway had brought a new import - dead bodies.

"Woking Heath, a large expanse of common land, is about three miles from the town, and on it has been formed the large cemetery (opened in 1854) belonging to the London Necropolis Company. It is laid out with great taste: and the little chapels are good specimens in miniature of the Gothic style... Hearses are provided by the South-Western Railway Company, and a portion of the London station is specially set apart for the reception of the corpses."

WOTTON

Tree planter

"Methinks I still hear, sure that I still feel the dismal groans of our forests when that late dreadful hurricane subverted many thousands of great oaks, prostrating the trees, laying them in ghastly postures, like whole regiments fallen in battle by the sword of the conqueror, and crushing all that grew beneath them."

Hurricane? What hurricane? In this case that of November 26th, 1703, presaging our experience of October 1987. The writer was one of the great Surrey tree-lovers, John Evelyn, then near the end of his long life, and living in the Evelyn house at Wotton where he was born in 1620.

He was a man who had been everywhere and done everything - for his time. He had travelled on the continent, held office under Charles II and James II, had planted gardens and woods and visited all the great houses and written a diary like his contemporary Pepys.

In Surrey he laid out the garden at Wotton (for his elder brother originally) and that at Albury, for the Duke of Northumberland (see page 11) - and he planted trees. Surrey's weald clay had always been a home for oaks, but centuries of iron-smelting and ship-building had seriously reduced the oaks by Evelyn's time, while other large tracts of Surrey were open sandy heathland. Evelyn, through his travels, came across types of tree new to England and introduced them. The Scots pine and later the larch turned out to be splendidly suited to Surrey's sandy soils. The 1703 hurricane must have added to the impetus to plant and replant. As a result, West Surrey is almost symbolised by the Scots pine.

John Betjeman's Surrey poems are infused by its perfume:

> "Over the redolent pinewoods, in at the bathroom casement
> One fine Saturday, Windlesham bells shall call...."

Now that Surrey commoners no longer graze their animals on the sandy heaths, the trees are dominant. So much so that the National Trust has to defend Witley Common from total invasion by trees and its conversion to woods, so that a little of the old Surrey heathland may remain. But as a useful crop, the conifer flourished. A Board of Agriculture report of 1794 describes the effect of planting 12 acres of Crooksbury Heath with 4-foot Scots pine in 1776. In 12 years they were 14 feet high, and the first thinnings were taken; in 1794, when a second thinning was taken, they were 40 feet high

John Evelyn is also credited with encouraging hedge-planting, and in particular yew hedges and topiary. He helped to introduce all kinds of evergreens into the garden scene, and wrote practical guidance for the year's work in the garden - for his gardener to carry out.

King John and the Pope

A national crisis in which Britain was pitted against the bureaucracy of Europe ? It sounds familiar, but this was in the reign of King John, and commemorated in stone in the little church of Wotton.

John's relations with the Church were not good, and in 1205 he had a row with the monks of Canterbury over the election of a new Archbishop. It was after all a top job in the state. The Pope (Innocent III) called in to decide, eventually chose Stephen Langton - who was at least English - but after Stephen was consecrated in Italy he was forced to remain abroad for six years. As a result, Innocent laid an interdict on John's kingdom which lasted until 1213.

During this time the services of the church in England were severely curtailed. There was no proper Christian burial, and there were no marriages in church. Sermons were preached in churchyards, the dead buried under hedges. Bishops protested, but for their own safety fled abroad. John retaliated by seizing church property, and antagonising the church still more.

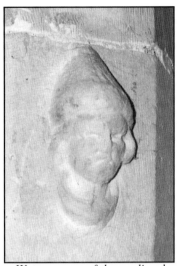

Wotton - one of the medieval carved heads in the porch

Then in 1209 the King was himself excommunicated; this meant that to have dealings with him imperilled your immortal soul, and it became the duty of other Christian kings to invade England and depose him. With France ready to oblige, King John gave in, by means of a ceremony before the Pope's legate, in which his kingdoms were resigned to the Pope and received back from him in fealty. It also meant that he had to accept Stephen Langton as Archbishop and compensate a lot of despoiled clergy.

In a small Surrey church, then new, these momentous times were depicted in stone, by means of a set of eight portrait heads carved over the south doorway. They show Pope, King, Queen, Baron, Priest, Peasant, Archbishop and Papal Legate, and are thought to be carved about 1215-1216.

Stephen Langton is an important name in these parts, but his association with this part of Surrey is more legend than history. A 19th century historical romance ("Stephen Langton" by Martin Tupper) even involves him in a love interest with a nun. A 1934 pageant at Abinger has him (fictionally) visiting the church there. That has been enough to cause the restaurant at Friday Street to be named after him. In real life he was

95

certainly prominent in trying to hold the ring between John and the rebellious barons at the time of Magna Carta, when our carved Wotton heads were new. They mercifully escaped being chopped off by Puritan image-breakers, having been earlier covered by a layer of plaster, where they stayed unseen until being rediscovered in the "restoration" in the nineteenth century.

The church also holds the tombs and monuments of the Evelyn family, one of whose homes was Wotton Manor, a short distance away on the other side of the A25.